A BRIEF HISTORY OF
THE UNIVERSITY OF
SOUTHWESTERN LOUISIANA
1900 to 1960

by

Florent Hardy, Jr., Ph.D.

Baton Rouge
Claitor's Publishing Division

Published and for sale by:
CLAITOR'S PUBLISHING DIVISION
3653 Perkins Road, PO BOX 261333
Baton Rouge, LA 70826

DEDICATION

In Memory
of
Capt. Arthur Joseph delaHoussaye, III USMCR
(USL BA '65)

and all other Alumni and former students of
Southwestern who gave their lives in service to their
country.

An aerial view of Southwestern's Campus

Southwestern Archives

FOREWORD AND ACKNOWLEDGEMENTS

This study is different from anything previously written about the history of the University of Southwestern Louisiana. It is a brief narrative survey of all aspects of Southwestern's history inclusive of the founding of the Industrial Institute (1900), the educational growth of the Industrial's high school program (1900-1920), and the Southwestern Louisiana Institute of Liberal and Technical Learning, (1921-1960). The Southwestern Archives and Manuscripts Collection made possible utilization of original source material not previously available.

The author wishes to express thanks to Glenn Abel, Robert Angelle, Thomas Arceneaux, James S. Bonnet, A. Wilmot Dalferes, Joel L. Fletcher, Kenneth B. Hait, Drayton Lewis, Joseph Riehl, Miss Pearl Segura, and Alexander G. Urban for the interviews which provided information essential to this work.

The author also expresses appreciation to Mrs. Lydia Gajan Daigreport, Mrs. Mayo Blanchet, Miss Pearl Segura and Glenn Conrad for their assistance.

Special thanks goes to Dr. Henry C. Dethloff, Advisor to the author, Dr. James H. Dormon and Dr. Vincent H. Cassidy.

This work could not have been written without the moral support of the author's family and friends. Mrs. Edith A. Calais, aunt of the author, greatly helped with unending moral support.

INTRODUCTION

In 1900 an institution of higher learning for southwest Louisiana residents was established in Lafayette, Louisiana. Through its first sixty years two great changes occurred,

> the development of a mere high school into a liberal arts college (1921) and the transition from an institution of liberal and technical learning to a full-fledged university (1960).

The Southwestern Archives and Manuscripts Collection which contains the official records of the University supplemented by personal interviews made this narrative history of Southwestern possible. This work is different from any other survey of Southwestern's history in that it is not merely a statistical survey, but a narrative account of the academic and administrative history of the University of Southwestern Louisiana.

Southwestern's transition from an industrial institute to a liberal arts college (1921) into a full-fledged university (1960) can be attributed heavily to the strong academic foundations laid by Edwin Lewis Stephens between 1900 and 1938, the physical growth sponsored by Lether Frazar before World War II, and the solid academic developments of the Fletcher administration as well as to the support of area citizens and a dedicated faculty. Just as no person can live without nourishment, no respectable university can exist without the continuous upgrading of its present academic structure.

TABLE OF CONTENTS

Scenic Cypress Lake is the "heart" of Southwestern's Campus.
Southwestern Archives

The youngest in the sisterhood of State institutions of learning, the Southwestern Louisiana Industrial Institute, will begin its first session this month with every promise of an eminently successful career. Starting out with the strongest financial and moral support of the people where it is located; domiciled in buildings which, for excellence of architectural workmanship and adaptability to educational requirements, are unsurpassed by any in the State; provided in its various departments with a full and well selected equipment; and born in the most auspicious era of our State's history, her star just rising from beyond the horizon sheds forth a light full of promise and hope.

New Orleans <u>Daily States</u>
September 1, 1901

CHAPTER 1

THE FORMATIVE YEARS

In 1898 few could aspire to an education in southwest Louisiana above the elementary level.[1] Indeed, in the state at large, many children had little opportunity to obtain any education. The nineteenth-century idea in Louisiana that education was basically unessential for economic progress retarded the development of public school systems. Many believed that education was necessary only for the governing classes. In the Catholic area, it was believed that the Church rather than the State should educate the children, thus further decreasing the demand for public schools. Only 48.5% of the 404,757 educable youth of Louisiana received any educational training during the last decade of the nineteenth century.[2] Approximately 38.5% of both white and Negro Louisiana residents over ten years old were illiterate in 1900.[3]

The lack of adequate educational facilities in southwest Louisiana contributed to Louisiana's high illiteracy rate. Lafayette Parish Superintendent of Education Claude Francois Latiolais' biennial report shows that in Lafayette Parish there were 35 teachers employed in 29 public schools with an attendance of 1,037 students during the school year 1896-97. Student enrollment rose slowly. In 1898 there were 1,646 white students and 230 Negro students taught by 35 white teachers and 2 Negro teachers. In 1900, 1,060 white students and 206 Negro students were taught by 38 white and 2 Negro teachers.[4] There was no high school in Lafayette Parish and no college in southwest Louisiana.

The founding of the Southwestern Louisiana Industrial Institute stems from the determined efforts of Robert Martin and others interested in improving the underdeveloped educational system of southwest Louisiana. Martin, born in Breaux Bridge, Louisiana, in 1853, received his formal education from a St. Martinville parochial school, a New Orleans high school and commercial school, and the Louisiana State University. Upon completing his formal

Senator Robert Martin, Louisiana Senator who first introduced the
bill (1896) which later established Southwestern (1900).

Southwestern Archives

education, Senator Martin studied law in St. Martinville under the guidance of his uncle Alcibiades deBlanc, Justice of the Supreme Court of Louisiana, and was subsequently admitted to the Louisiana Bar.

Martin, a successful attorney and a prosperous businessman, was elected to the Louisiana Senate in 1896 from the thirteenth legislative district which consisted of the Parishes of Iberia, Lafayette, and St. Martin.[5] In Senator Martin's first year in the Senate, Governor Murphy J. Foster appointed him to a legislative committee which was "to visit the state institutions of higher education, and to report upon their conditions and needs."[6] The findings of the committee's study revealed to Senator Martin the need for an institution of higher learning in his legislative district for the benefit of all of southwest Louisiana.

Martin's determination to provide an institution of higher learning for his section of the state[7] resulted in the introduction of a bill in 1896 "to create and establish an Industrial Institute and Academy for the education of the white children of the State of Louisiana in arts and sciences," which passed both House and Senate.[8] The original bill was vetoed by Governor Foster because of insufficient funds, but he promised executive approval if the bill were re-enacted and passed in the 1898 legislative session.[9]

The act to create and establish an Industrial Institute for southwest Louisiana was again presented in the 1898 legislative session. At first there was difficulty in passing the bill. A tie vote was broken with twenty-four yeas and eight nays after reconsideration of the bill's importance to southwest Louisiana. On July 13, 1898, the bill became law after receiving executive approval.[10]

Interest now focused on the most suitable location for the new Institute within the thirteenth legislative district (Iberia, Lafayette, and St. Martin Parishes). Serious competition developed over the location of the school. Committees representing the people of Lafayette, New Iberia, and Scott prepared statements for presentation to the Board of

Trustees of SLII in support of their chosen location for the new Institute. The proposal of the committee from Lafayette as presented by Chairman Charles D. Caffery represented the Lafayette area as "the geographical and actual center of southwest Louisiana with unusual railroad facilities,..." and as "one of the most thickly settled Parishes in the State." The people of Lafayette also accepted a special property tax of two mills to donate to the Institute for ten years.[11]

New Iberia's[12] proposal was based on the offer of land "picturesquely beautiful, and from a sanitary standpoint well drained and healthy,... a five mill tax of all property assessments within its corporation for a period of ten years commencing with the year 1900, and fifty acres of land,... and a desirable location because of the availability of the Southern Pacific Railroad."[13]

Alcide Judice, a Scott businessman, offered 100 arpents of land or $50,000 to the Board of Trustees of the Institute if Scott were chosen as the site of the new school.[14]

The eight member Board of Trustees of SLII appointed by Governor Foster met for an organizational meeting on January 3, 1900. At this meeting the Board elected Edwin Lewis Stephens as the Institute's first president.[15]

At the first executive session of the Board of Trustees on January 5, 1900, Robert Martin moved that Lafayette be chosen as the location of the Institute. Martin's motion stemmed from the immediate availability of $18,000 from private donations and $10,000 advance on the proposed property tax by the citizens of Lafayette from the First National Bank and the Bank of Lafayette. Lafayette's financial contribution easily surpassed New Iberia's pledge of $5,000 and Scott's pledge of $8,000.[16]

On May 15, 1900, Lafayette was chosen by the Board of Trustees by a five to two vote as the location for the Southwestern Louisiana Industrial Institute. In 1900, Lafayette, with a population of 3,500 was an important agricultural center being the "junction-point of the chief industrial interests of Louisiana – those of sugar, cotton and rice."[17] The main reasons for the choice of Lafayette by the Board of Trustees were summed up in a statement by Governor Murphy J. Foster:

First, the donation of twenty-five acres of land beautifully situated, the gift of a private citizen, valued at $2,500.

Second, a cash bonus subscribed by the citizens of Lafayette of $5,000.

Third, a cash bonus of the police jury of the Parish of Lafayette, of $3,000, and

Fourth, an annual tax of two mills on the dollar on the assessed valuation of the property of the Parish of Lafayette for ten years.[18]

The new Institute was to be located on a tract of land just outside of the Lafayette city limits donated to the Institute by Mrs. Maxim E. Girard and her son, Crow Girard, President of the Bank of Lafayette.[19]

The choice of Lafayette by the Board of Trustees was, according to one newspaper account, "hailed with delight," as the residents of southwest Louisiana realized that "the establishment of this school…was a most potential factor in education, as well as material advancement of the country.[20] The organization of Lafayette's new educational facility now became the responsibility of the Institute's first President, Edwin L. Stephens.

President Stephens was responsible for the organizational problems and the quality of education offered by the Institute. His primary duty, the presentation of potential faculty members to the Board of Trustees, required discreet evaluation. The first faculty of the Institute chosen by the Board included:

Victor Leander Roy.. Science
Ashby Woodson...Manual Training
Miss Gertrude Mayfield................................Domestic Science

Miss Edith G. Dupré .... English and French
Florent Sontag ....Music
L. W. Mayer.. Stenography
Mrs. Elizabeth Fowles   Matron of the Girls'
Baker .... Dormitory[21]

His duty also included the seeking of appropriations for maintenance, and for the construction of necessary buildings on the campus. The appropriation required for the operation through April 30, 1902, totaled $79,343.98: $41,939.05 for the Main Building, $19,588.97 for a dormitory for young ladies, $11,541.76 for furniture and fixtures, and $6,274.20 for salaries.[22] These include only the major items needed and salaries.

Stephens sent the newspapers throughout the State an advertisement of the facilities of the new Institute which stated that Southwestern Louisiana Industrial Institute, created by the Louisiana Legislature, was for the education of both boys and girls. The Industrial Institute offered courses in English, French, mathematics, history, science, bookkeeping, stenography, drawing, gymnastics, music and manual training, and courses in wood and iron for boys and domestic economy for girls. Girls lived on campus and paid $12.50 a month for board. Boys lived with private families in town for a minimum of $10 a month. Tuition was free for all students, but incidental fees of $4 per session for school activities were charged. Free tuition encouraged an increased enrollment while incidental fees provided for the maintenance of educational equipment used by the students.[23] Children over the age of fourteen with a minimum of a sixth grade education would be admitted. Thus the institute began as essentially a high school.

The name of the Southwestern Louisiana Industrial Institute included in its title "Industrial" to emphasize "the motor and creative activities of hand and brain,..."[24] and "to meet the great and increasing demand that...existed in South Louisiana for industrial education and manual training."[25] Because of the existing importance of industrial education in Louisiana, the Institute offered four industrial courses and one academic course. The courses offered at the Institute for the first session were the four-year Academic course, the three-year Manual Training and Domestic Science courses, the two-year Stenography and Typewriting course, and the one-year Commercial course.[26]

During the first sessions at the Institute the people of Lafayette wanted higher education, but they also wanted the Industrial Institute to be more easily accessible to younger students. An editorial of the Lafayette *Advertiser* praised the Institute and the "best management possible," yet criticized the entrance requirement of a sixth grade education stating that the lowering of the standard requirement of admission "would at an early day fill the Institute."[27] President Stephens replied to this question of the Institute's standard of admission by inviting all interested parents to visit the Institute. He welcomed discussion of existing admission requirements.[28] He maintained that quality, not quantity, was vital to the educational growth of Southwestern.

By the end of 1901 the Main Building, the Girls Dormitory, and the Workshop[29] had been completed. President Stephens described the new Main Building as "this temple of a people's hope, this ever enduring symbol of their faith in the high destiny which awaits their children's children, this altar of a noble sacrifice for the sake of mankind."[30] This "temple" was a "two story and a basement brick structure...." It consisted of an assembly hall, to seat five hundred pupils, and eighteen classrooms."[31]

The dormitory for girls was the second building constructed on the campus. The local newspaper described it as

an excellent two-story brick building,...to afford accommodation when fully completed for eighty persons. The first floor...consisted of seven dormitory rooms, a bathroom, the reception room, the Matron's room, the kitchen, and two store rooms; all of which...were adequately furnished. The second floor interior...had provisions for...twenty-eight girls.[32]

7

Old Martin Hall (1900-1963), Southwestern's first building described by President Edwin L. Stephens as "the temple of a people's hope...this altar of a noble sacrifice for the sake of mankind," was named in honor of Robert Martin who was responsible for Southwestern's establishment.

Southwestern Archives

The workshop, a single-story building, housed industrial education and manual training facilities. It contained "equipment for work in wood" and "a space reserved for a forge shop," and was built to provide for future expansion.[33]

The Institute opened on September 18, 1901.[34] On the first day 100 students appeared for classes. This number increased by the end of the session to a then impressive total of 145 students, 50 girls and 95 boys.[35]

No students completed course work in 1902. In place of graduation exercises at the end of the Institute's first session, the students and faculty presented a week-long ceremony commemorating the completion of the first school year of the Institute. A concert by the Music department, an exhibit of the industrial and manual products of the students, a display of the students' writings by the English department, and the exhibit of chemistry experiments were part of the festivities. Visitors learned of the formation of a football and a baseball team, the organization of the Attakapas Literary Society, the formation of a glee club, and the organization of a Young Ladies' Basketball Club, all of which were a vital part of the extra-curricular activities begun during the first session at the Institute.[36] Jefferson Caffery, a noted American diplomat, was a member of this first-year class at Southwestern.

During the first session the students represented twelve parishes and two states, Louisiana and Texas.[37] The people of the Lafayette area wholeheartedly supported the students of Southwestern. President Stephens described the moral and financial support of Lafayette's citizens as "the greatest local support to the establishment of a State institution of learning that...had ever been given in this section of the country...."[38] Such support generated enthusiasm and school spirit among the students, who unsuccessfully petitioned for the compulsory wearing of uniforms by all students to "attract-attention,..." and to place the students "under the solicitous (surveillance) of the friends of education and of the Institute."[39]

9

Although President Stephens refused to permit the students to wear uniforms to "attract-attention," he encouraged student-group participation in numerous extracurricular activities. For example, he spearheaded the organization of a semi-monthly school newspaper.[40] The paper began publication during the second session. The first publication of *The Vermilion*, as the paper was named, consisted of general news and class notes. This "bright college paper" became the voice of the students and was sold by subscription for fifty cents per school year.[41]

Extra-curricular activities contributed to the early development of a school-type environment at the Institute. Regulation of the students' activities was also vital to the proper functioning of the Institute. The administration made and enforced rules for the regulation of the students. The young men of the Institute were

> placed upon their honor not to go into a saloon, not to take any intoxicating drink, to observe the hours of study in their respective boarding-places, and to conform to such other disciplinary regulations as may be required of them as students.[42]

Strict disciplinary rules also governed the female students living on the campus. They were required to report to the Matron of the dormitory when leaving and returning to the campus. Girls were not permitted to spend the night away from the dormitory unless chaperoned by their parents. Friday afternoons, and Sundays for church services were the only times women students were allowed to visit town.[43]

Ten students comprised the first graduating class of the Institute. These students received diplomas for completion of the Academic course. Governor William W. Heard and Lieutenant Governor Albert Estopinial were among the prominent persons present during Southwestern's first commencement week held in May, 1903. Addresses on the importance of education as well as the presence of

Southwestern's first graduating class (1903). Front row (l. to r.): William Parkerson Mills, Pothier J. Voorhies, Harold Demanade, and Henry DeKoven Smedes. Back row: Alma L. Gulley, Maxim A. Beraud, Edith Trahan, and Annie T. Bell and Rhena Boudreaux. Not pictured is Jacques Domengeaux.

Southwestern Archives

distinguished guests made the commencement ceremony impressive to the visitors, many of whom were given the opportunity to attend the exercises through the special-rate tickets of the Southern Pacific Railroad.[44]

The Institute began its third session in September 1903 with a 25% increase in enrollment over the session of 1902-03.[45] The enrollment reached a total of 220 students as compared to the enrollment of 145 in 1901, and 180 in 1902.[46] According to the administration, the Institute had become "a rallying point for the educational forces of the surrounding country, a challenge to those who feared self-taxation for education, and an objective point for the children of all the lower schools."[47]

President Stephens added two new courses to the curriculum in the 1903-04 session. The demand for telegraphers by railroad companies during the formative years of the Institute led Stephens, a one-time telegrapher for the Iowa Central Railroad,[48] to include a two-year course of Telegraphy to the curriculum.[49]

A course in agriculture was also added to the curriculum during the 1903-04 session. Reflecting a nationwide interest in vocational agricultural training this new course permitted

> students in the third year of the regular manual training department, of taking up the pursuit of agricultural subjects, instead of manual subjects,...preparing the students more fully for taking intelligent part in the agricultural development of the country.[50]

During the 1903-04 session the graduates of the Institute organized the Alumni Association of the Southwestern Industrial Institute. The Association's purpose was "to promote good fellowship among its members, to strengthen the ties of loyalty and devotion to their Alma Mater and at all times to further the interests of the Institute."[51] Membership in the Association was open to any SLII graduate. Members met at the end of each session at which time each paid fifty cents dues. Officers of the Association included President, a Vice President from each class, Secretary, Treasurer, and an Alumni Orator whose duty was to give the commencement address.[52]

To increase the participation in sports and literary activities among the schools of southwest Louisiana, the Interscholastic Athletic and Oratorical Association was organized in the spring of 1904 under the directorship of Jesse W. S. Lillibridge, a member of the faculty at the Institute.[53] The purpose of this Association was the "development and improvement of Amateur Athletics, Oratory, and Vocal Music...."[54] The IAOA's first event was held at Southwestern on April 16, 1904, and marked the founding of a literary and athletic competition among area schools which continues to the present.

President Stephens realized the importance of a well disciplined program of activities for the young men students while they attended the Institute. His experience with military discipline while he attended LSU encouraged him to want military discipline at the Institute. As a result Southwestern fulfilled the military requirements of the Department of the Army and was assigned a Commander of Cadets.[55] Although Southwestern was not a land grant college and thus not required to maintain military training, the University has since 1904 maintained a military corps on its campus.

The main objectives of military discipline, as described by Stephens, were to discipline in lessons centered on "obedience, self control, and respect for authority."[56] In 1904 the Cadet system was praised by the Administration as having already reaped improved "habits of neatness, promptness, order, regularity as well as in giving a strong, wholesome tone to discipline."[57]

The commencement of 1904 was similar to the three previous commencement exercises. Activities during commencement week included the annual inspection of the exhibits from the Industrial and Manual Training Departments, a concert by the Music Department, and the commencement ceremony.[58]

The fourth annual session began with a record enrollment of 157 students,[59] and this number increased to 250 by the end of the session.[60] This increase in enrollment produced a need for a men's dormitory. Through President Stephens' efforts, preparations were completed to give the Girls Dormitory to the boys and build a new dormitory for the girls.[61]

The increased enrollment also led to the establishment of a set of regulations for the morning bell. All students were to leave the building during recess and immediately after the afternoon dismissal bell. The students were to "march from class room to class room quietly," and without talking.[62] Disciplinary measures have really changed during Southwestern's history.

The students were on a merit system in order for the Institute to enforce its regulations. Dismissal from school was the punishment for any student who received one hundred demerits.[63] During the fourth session President Stephens refused permission to the parents of a student who wished to visit town with her friends by simply stating, "It is contrary to our rules."[64] In another case, President Stephens wrote to the parents of a student who disobeyed the restriction of confinement to his dormitory room: "I therefore see no other course to pursue than an order announcing his peremptory dismissal from the Institute, for desertion."[65]

By 1905 the strict military discipline on campus caused some of the young men to attempt to move off campus to board in town. They desired to be free from the compulsory military discipline regulations while attending school. President Stephens saw these desires of the young men as attempts to dodge

the restraints and duties of the military system of discipline-which requires them to get up promptly at a certain time, to clean up their rooms for inspection, to be punctual at their meals, their studies, and their exercises, to go to bed and put 'lights out' at 10 p.m., to be orderly in every way and to stay right on the Institute grounds except when specifically permitted to go out.[66]

Foster Hall was named in honor of a Southwest Louisiana family of which Louisiana Governor Murphy J. Foster was a member. Foster Hall was the first dormitory for girls and when it was replaced by DeClouet it became the first men's dorm.

Southwestern Archives

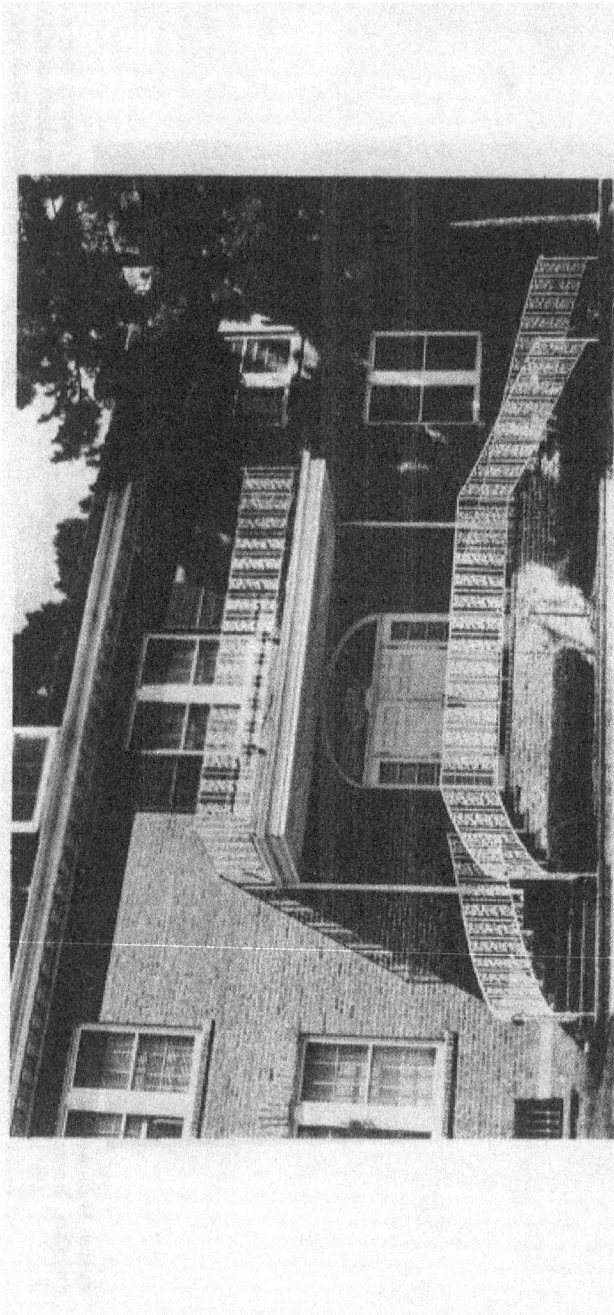

DeClouet Hall was one of the first buildings on Southwestern's campus. It was a girl's dormitory named in honor of a Southwest Louisiana family.

Southwestern Archives

In order to maintain the rules placed on the activities of the male students, President Stephens required that all young men who attended the Institute other than Lafayette residents were to live on campus in the men's dormitory unless they lived with close relatives in town.[67] He did this to maintain close supervision over the young men students. At this time this was not unreasonable.

The growing demands of the Institute resulted in the increase in faculty and staff in 1905 to the following: the President; Professors in Science, Manual Training, Stenography, Music, English and French, Gymnastics, Commercial subjects, Latin, Mathematics, Domestic Science, Art, Geography, Drawing and Telegraphy; the Matron for the young Ladies, and the Matron for the young Men; the Librarian and the Secretary.[68]

The graduation of 1905 was shortened from a week-long event to a two-day ceremony. The commencement ceremony consisted of the annual inspection of exhibits of Domestic Science, Commerce, Stenography, Telegraphy, the Workshop and the Art Room,[69] as well as the actual commencement exercises.

By the end of the fourth school session, the growth of the Institute's curriculum had expanded from the original five courses offered to seven individual courses of study, including the courses in Telegraphy and Agriculture.

The first seven years of the Industrial Institute's operation were a boost to southwest Louisiana's educational growth. In fact, by 1905, 62 students finished course work at the Institute.[70] The organizers of the Institute's educational program headed by President Edwin L. Stephens provided the white citizens of southwest Louisiana with educational opportunities previously non-existent.

By providing practical education in academic, industrial, and manual training, regulated by strict military discipline, SLII established itself as an important educational institution accessible to virtually all white persons interested in furthering their schooling. By 1905 the Southwestern

Louisiana Industrial Institute, still basically a high school, had marked the beginning of a new era in public education in southwest Louisiana.

Edwin Lewis Stephens, Southwestern's first president, as a young man.
Southwestern Archives

CHAPTER II

THE INDUSTRIAL INSTITUTE

Edwin Lewis Stephens, who guided the Industrial Institute during its formative years, was the son of Joseph Henry Stephens and Isabelle Carolina Whitfield. Stephens was born on November 27, 1872, in Stephens Mill, Louisiana, a small town near Natchitoches, Louisiana. He received his formal elementary education from the private school of William C. Jack in Natchitoches and attended Keatchie College in De Soto Parish where he studied academic and commercial courses, including telegraphy, for five years, (1883-1888). Upon completion of course work at Keatchie, Stephens joined the railroad in Marshalltown, Iowa, as a telegraph operator and relief agent. He stayed in Iowa only one year because of his father's determination that his formal education be continued; thus, Stephens entered Louisiana State University in Baton Rouge in 1889, while working part time as telegraph operator for the Texas and Pacific Railroad.

In 1892 he graduated from Louisiana State University, and in the summer following his graduation he attended the Summer School of Methods in Glens Falls, New York, in preparation for a job at Louisiana Normal in Natchitoches where he was hired as an Instructor of Latin and Science.

While at Louisiana Normal, Stephens assisted in organizing the Louisiana Teachers' Association. In 1893, he attended Sauveur Summer School of Languages in Rockford, Illinois, and in 1894 he attended Harvard Summer School. When Stephens was not busy studying, he assisted in conducting teacher institutes held throughout Louisiana, as in Abbeville, Colfax, New Roads, Marksville, and St. Francisville.[1]

Stephens received the Helen Gould Scholarship to New York University in 1892. The requirements for qualification as a recipient of this scholarship were a four-year college degree with four years of teaching experience. The recipient always was required to be a resident along the line of the Texas and Pacific Railroad. This scholarship was to be awarded preferentially to sons or daughters of employees of the railroad.

Stephens possessed these qualifications,[2] and became the recipient of this valuable award.

In 1897 Stephens received his Master of Pedagogy degree from New York University, and in 1899 he received his Doctor of Pedagogy degree from the same University. His thesis topic was "The Public School System of Louisiana: An Account of Its Beginning and Recent Development, with a Critical Examination of its Organization and the Course of Study."[3] Stephens returned to Louisiana and became an Instructor of physics and chemistry at Boys High School (presently Warren Easton) in New Orleans.[4]

The Board of Trustees unanimously elected Edwin Lewis Stephens as the Industrial Institute's first president on January 3, 1900. His initial responsibility was to develop Southwestern's faculty, student enrollment, curriculum, and buildings during the Institute's formative years.

In 1902, President Stephens married Miss Beverly Randolph, an instructor of Drawing and Gymnastics. President and Mrs. Stephens became parents of three daughters: Beverly Randolph Stephens (1904), Caroline Parham Stephens (1907), and Margaret Fitz Randolph Stephens (1912).[5]

Stephens soon became deeply involved in statewide educational activities. He became President of the Louisiana Teachers' Association in 1905, editor of the *Louisiana School Review* in 1905, a participant in the Bureau of University Travel on a tour of Europe in 1907, and Professor of History of Education at the Summer School of the South held at the University of Tennessee in 1909. President Stephens' reputation as an educator spread outside of Louisiana. As a result of this he was offered the position of Editor in the United States Bureau of Education. This position he declined in favor of remaining at Southwestern.[6]

Stephens remained at Southwestern for thirty-eight years. Several times during this long presidency the Board of Trustees showed a vote of confidence in retaining Stephens as

21

president of Southwestern. The first of these instances occurred in 1912 when President Stephens was retained by a vote of confidence by the Board of Trustees of Southwestern after political rumor that he might be replaced. The Board's vote of confidence ended these meaningless rumors. It was stated in a New Orleans newspaper that Stephens'

> dismissal at this time for political reasons would have been unjust to him and to the people who have collaborated with him in developing the institution.[7]

The Lafayette *Gazette* stated:

> The people of Lafayette wish no change in the head of the Institute, and wisely so. Dr. Stephens is a man of high literary attainments, a practical and successful educator, an able executive, organizer and promoter.[8]

The people of the Lafayette area admired President Stephens as an educational leader. He was also a civic leader. Stephens became an enthusiastic supporter of the United States' participation in World War I. Because of his influence among the people of the Lafayette area, he was made the Chairman of the War Savings Stamps Drive in 1918; Chairman of the Salvation Army Drive in 1919, and Chairman of the Lafayette Parish Red Cross which collected $6,158.10 over its $10,000 quota during the War.[9] Stephens was also influential in organizing the Student Army Training Corps at Southwestern during the War.

Throughout his presidency, Stephens worked with the people of Lafayette. In 1924 as a result of his civic activity, he was elected President of the Lafayette Rotary Club. He also became the president of the Louisiana Library Association in 1925. In 1929 the Southwestern faculty further honored President Stephens for his devotion to education by presenting him with life membership in the National Education Association. During this year, Stephens also became a member of the Committee on International Relations with the NEA.[10]

Stephens sought to improve the social, economic, and educational welfare of the people of southwest Louisiana. By striving to improve educational opportunities for all white southwest Louisiana residents through Southwestern, he simultaneously desired to aid the progress of the city of Lafayette and civic progress, he stated, would be produced more successfully through increased taxation of Lafayette's citizens. Of course, no overwhelming approval was given this idea. Above all, Stephens recognized that "the fundamental requirement for all social or community progress is COOPERATION."[11] He followed this principle of "cooperation" in faculty relations.

In a practical application of this concern for progress, Stephens decided that he would personally instruct men from the southwest Louisiana area who were unable to read and write or speak English. This he did to "diminish the proportion of illiteracy..."[12] in Lafayette Parish and all of southwest Louisiana and prepare the residents of this area for a more enlightened future. Stephens made plans to offer adult education classes without charge to interested adults of the Lafayette area. Afternoon classes were to be held at Southwestern beginning on December 19, 1905, and continuing on succeeding Tuesdays and Thursdays on the campus.[13]

Southwestern Louisiana Industrial Institute was a response to a need in southwest Louisiana for educational development and industrial and academic training. As a result of the educational progress made by the Industrial Institute during its formative years, a Crowley newspaper praised Southwestern as

one of the most notable institutions of its class in the South. Practical, useful education... its mission.[14]

Southwestern was

located in one of the oldest, most densely populated sections of rural Louisiana, a section which had long been comparatively neglected by the State educationally speaking....[15]

Southwestern's educational importance in both manual and academic training during its formative years was briefly stated in a Chicago newspaper:

The institute…is not a mere labor school, designed to out servants; it is one of those manual training schools which turn out well-rounded men and women by cultivating hand and mind together.[16]

Enthusiastic support by the people of southwest Louisiana benefitted Southwestern in gaining rapid and steady growth. A memorandum on October 2, 1914, exemplifies the enthusiasm among the Lafayette residents in support of Southwestern.

At its next session the Legislature will be urged to pass a law compelling all able bodied citizens within walking distance of Lafayette to visit the Institute once each year.[17]

This shows the extreme but somewhat curious idealism of Southwestern's boosters.

President Stephens constantly strove to improve Southwestern's educational standards. For the 1907-08 session, a student desiring to enroll at Southwestern was required to have a seventh grade education, an increase of one grade level since Southwestern's establishment. This was the first such action in changing entrance requirements and it resulted in a decrease in enrollment from 262 for the 1906-07 session to 244 for the 1907-08 session.[18] The minimum age requirement of fourteen was also removed in 1907 provided that the potential student was capable of entering the third year class.[19]

The new entrance requirements displeased some of the local people; however, President Stephens argued that the entrance requirements for Southwestern were not "too high." He argued that the total enrollment of Southwestern was not a measure of the quality of her students. He also firmly stated that Southwestern was a special school in that it provided a wide range of studies and was not a Lafayette High School with entrance requirements favorable exclusively to students from Lafayette Parish.[20] Again in 1910 President Stephens announced a change in entrance requirements. He stated:

> I have planned to improve our principal course of study at the Industrial Institute by raising the standards of admission and graduation to a point of one half-year higher than what it was during the past session.[21]

Stephens further stated:

> This change is to strengthen the Institute as a State institution, making its courses more attractive to students from other sections of the State than southwest Louisiana.[22]

It was also agreed in 1910 that the standard of admission would be raised one complete term beginning with the fall session of 1912-13.[23] In 1912 new regulations provided that Southwestern graduates who had been previously admitted to the freshman class of Louisiana State University would now be admitted to the sophomore class.[24] Criticism and complaints from the area residents who favored permitting younger students to enter SLII usually followed increases in the minimum grade requirement as in 1907, 1910, and 1912. Stephens consistently argued that no sacrifice to the quality of Southwestern's students was being made;[25] instead, he stated that Southwestern was increasing its minimum grade requirements to improve its educational standards.

The standard entrance requirement was again raised from ninth to a tenth grade minimum for the 1916-17 session.[26] By 1917 Southwestern was a junior college. It provided educational training comparable to the last two years of high school and the first two years of college[27] to students enrolled prior to the 1916-17 session. The last year of high school and two years of college courses were offered to students enrolled after the 1916-17 session. Success in upgrading the Institute can largely be attributed to Stephens' personal dedication and perseverance.

By the 1920-21 session Southwestern offered a complete four-year college course and became the Southwestern Louisiana Institute of Liberal and Technical Learning. The college courses offered by Southwestern this first session included

> arts and sciences, agriculture and mechanic arts, teacher training for work in the elementary grades and high school, and teacher training in home economics.[28]

The curriculum was gradually expanded with emphasis on a more practical education for students of south Louisiana.[29] The provisions for a course in agriculture including both class work and actual training in the field was an initial step in this direction.

Southwest Louisiana has always been a rich agricultural area. Farmers had long emphasized the importance of agricultural training for young men. Because of the prevailing importance of agricultural training, President Stephens announced the preparation for a government Demonstration Farm at Southwestern.[30] The Demonstration Farm was an outgrowth of agricultural experimentation work during the early 1900s by Dr. Seaman A. Knapp, Special Agent for the Promotion of Agriculture in the South. This was a federal agency working to provide more efficient farming methods to the southern farmer. Development of agricultural experiment farms served to demonstrate that efficient agricultural production could be obtained through

> good management, by up-to-date methods of seed selection and cultivation, and particularly by careful rotation diversification of crops, an important phase of farming improvement in Louisiana.[31]

By December 1907, thirty acres were under cultivation on Southwestern's Demonstration Farm located on campus and conducted by the Bureau of Plant Industry of the United

States Department of Agriculture.[32] The agriculture course directed by Mr. Jordan G. Lee, Jr. acted on Dr. Knapp's theory that, "What a man hears he may doubt; what he sees, he may possibly doubt, but what he does himself, he cannot doubt."[33] It included

> the care, feeding and breeding of stock, the study and preparation of soils for planting, plant foods, fertilizers, planting, cultivation, harvesting, rotation of crops, modern methods and implements, drainage, truck farming and special study of crops adapted to this section.[34]

The agriculture course centered on the Demonstration Farm which was transferred from Knapp's original plan for the experimental farms in Terrell, Texas.

Emphasis on practical education is evident in Southwestern's curriculum which included the plan for a course in telegraphy as early as 1903-04. The actual offering of courses in telegraphy, however, did not begin until December 1907. The course, directed by an experienced telegraph operator, John I. Hulse, was arranged so that young people of the area who desired to become telegraph operators would be permitted to take courses in telegraphy with no other required subjects but mathematics and English. The telegraphy course presented the students with "minute practical details of every duty a telegraph operator has to perform."[35] The course was dropped from the curriculum in 1914 as a result of the cessation of the annual grant of $1,020 from the Southern Pacific Railway.[36] Thus, the study of telegraphy ended, but was temporarily re-started during World War I when a special course in radio and buzzer telegraphy for conscripts was held at Southwestern.[37]

The overall effect of World War I on Southwestern's curriculum was not of great consequence. The decrease in enrollment caused a temporary discontinuance of the Commercial Course.[38] In 1920 the Commercial Department, reorganized by Mr. Ralph Holden Agate, was again included in the curriculum after being excluded from the curriculum during the sessions of 1918 and 1919.[39]

27

Increasing demand by the students for commercial education in the mid-twenties resulted in Southwestern offering night courses in commerce which led to a Bachelor of Science degree. The courses offered were:

Expert bookkeeping, advanced accounting, business English, business law, business economics, salesmanship, labor problems, stenography, typewriting, railroad transportation problems, marketing problems, trade unionism.[40]

A strong demand for new courses by the students of Southwestern usually resulted in the addition of new courses to the curriculum, as was true in the case of the inclusion of music instruction at Southwestern. Although students were allowed to enroll for music instruction, they were required to pay certain fees not included in tuition fees. Similarly, in the early twenties, increasing interest arose among the students for a practical course in advertising and resulted in Southwestern adding an advertising course to its curriculum.[41]

Stephens also sought to add a teacher education program to the curriculum. As early as 1906 President Stephens began seeking a teacher training program for Southwestern. He stated in 1908:

My chief recommendation is a renewal of the recommendation I made in my last biennial report to enlarge the scope of the school by so reorganizing its curriculum as to include a thorough and complete course for the training of teachers.[42]

The State Normal College in Natchitoches opposed this proposal stating that one Normal school was sufficient for Louisiana. President Stephens argued, however, that the Normal in Lafayette would not harm Natchitoches; instead, it would aid southwest Louisiana and all of Louisiana by giving Louisiana educators employment in Louisiana schools in preference to out-of-state residents.[43] Stephens further argued to the State Board of Education:

It would only be wisdom on the part of the State to provide another place for teacher training, when it can be done without cost for buildings, grounds, equipment, organization, or any other cost except for a training teacher and two grade teachers.[44]

Southwestern finally was granted a summer Normal program because of its practicality.

Southwestern offered its first summer Normal (summer school for teachers) May 31 to July 31, 1906, under the direction of Professor Irving J. Foote. This course, open to teachers who held second and third grade certificates, was supplemented with a special course offered for first grade teachers. There were also provisions for a course given to persons who desired to take the examination for a teacher's certificate at the end of the summer session.[45]

A model school, organized in 1909 for practical education of persons taking summer normal courses, increased the efficiency of the Normal course. The model school consisted of thirty-six pupils in grades one through five. The goal of the Normal course was to provide the potential teachers with practical teaching experience.[46]

In response to a potential applicant for the summer Normal, Stephens made it clear that emphasis centered on the capability of the student. The course was "only for those…" who were "already seriously endeavoring to become teachers and who expect to try the examination for the certificate at the end of the session of Summer Normal School."[47]

In 1911 an announcement of new teacher education courses appeared. This announcement included teachers' courses in industrial education. The specific courses offered in the industrial education program were the Home and Farm Construction Work under the leadership of Harry Cuthbert Bond, and the Agriculture and School Gardening course under Miss Elizabeth B. Kelly. These were all one-year courses opened only to teachers who held a first or second grade certificate.[48]

The rapid growth of the Summer Normal at Southwestern necessitated the subdivision of the departments. Thus, in 1912 the Summer Normal was subdivided into the Industrial, Academic, and Pedagogic departments.[49]

Southwestern had completely organized and developed its teacher training program by 1912. The problem now was to have graduates of Southwestern accepted as qualified teachers by the school boards of the State without being given a Louisiana Teachers' Certificate.[50]

Stephens and other Southwestern administrators passed a resolution without the Board of Education's approval which provided that students of Southwestern completing the course of study in Teacher Training should be awarded "a First Grade Teachers' Certificate, valid for five years, without examination...."[51] This resolution which overextended Southwestern's administrative power displeased Superintendent Thomas H. Harris who wrote to Stephens, "You will be lucky now if your training department is not abolished altogether. You played the Devil!"[52] This action exemplifies President Stephens' determination and eventually boosted Southwestern's chances for a teacher training program.

The Price-Johnson Bill,[53] introduced to the Louisiana Legislature in 1914, asked that industrial institutions be given Normal departments. The bill proposed that Louisiana Industrial Institute (Ruston), Southwestern Louisiana Industrial Institute (Lafayette), and Louisiana State Normal School (Natchitoches) be given a department of Pedagogy consisting of nine month sessions offering courses in psychology, general and special education methods, classroom observation, and practice teaching as required by the State Board of Education. At first the bill failed. Stephens interpreted the defeat as the State Normal's victory:

merely to continue its present exclusive monopoly of the privilege of having its diploma carry a first grade certificate without any further examination.[54]

Finally, in 1915, State Superintendent Harris wrote to President Stephens telling him of the State Board of Education's approval of the proposed professional course of teacher training, and the exclusion of the examination for a teacher's certificate once this course was completed.[55]

President Stephens and other Southwestern administrators had proven that the State Normal in Natchitoches was not sufficient to meet Louisiana's need for qualified teachers. Thus, Stephens had been victorious in adding an approved teacher education course to Southwestern's curriculum.

The organization of the Summer Normal School was reviewed by the Southwestern administration in 1916. Changes made since 1912 were the addition of a two-year training course in elementary grades, a two-year training program in agriculture and farm mechanics for high school graduates, a two-year training course in home economics and household arts, a department of instruction in biology and bacteriology, a department of instruction in pedagogy and practice teaching with a model school of lower grades, and a department of instruction in dairying and animal husbandry.[56] As a result of the rapid growth of the curriculum in teaching training, Fuller M. Hamilton joined the faculty in 1917 to aid in assisting Professor Foote in the program.[57]

The addition of vocational education and a teacher training program characterized Southwestern's educational development as an institute of higher learning. President Stephens was virtually individually responsible for SLII's gradual conversion from a high school to a college. For the first forty years Stephen's leadership and foresight were important in providing the solid foundation upon which to build the institution into a full-fledged liberal arts college.

CHAPTER III

THE LIBERAL ARTS COLLEGE

The State Board of Education changed the name of the college from Southwestern Louisiana Industrial Institute to Southwestern Louisiana Institute of Liberal and Technical Learning in 1921. This change in name accompanied Southwestern's conversion from a high school-junior college institution to a four-year, degree-granting, liberal arts college. Stephens, who was irritated when persons mentioned Southwestern as an "Industrial" school, quickly corrected this misnomer by pointing out that Southwestern's name had been changed and that it was no longer an "Industrial" school but a liberal arts college.[1]

Although Southwestern became a four-year liberal arts college in 1921, it continued to offer high school training equivalent to the last two years of secondary education. The administration of Southwestern decided to segregate high school and college classes, and to drop half a year in the high school department at mid-term of every year until only college courses remained.[2]

The college curriculum included four main courses: the Literary course, the Home Economics course, the Education course, and the Agricultural Engineering course. Each was a specific course with specific requirements, as is indicated by the description in the Institute Bulletin, 1920-21. The literary course leading to the Bachelor of Arts Degree was a four-year course requiring two years of a foreign language. The home economics course was subdivided into the two-year course and the four-year course. Students completing the two-year course were issued a certificate, and a Bachelor of Science in Home Economics was conferred upon students completing the four-year course. The education course also consisted of a two-year and a four-year curriculum. As in home economics, students completing the two-year course were issued a certificate while a Bachelor of Science in Education was conferred upon students completing the four-year course. Completion of the four agricultural engineering course requirements entitled the student to a Bachelor of Science in Agricultural Engineering.[3]

There was no opposition from LSU stemming from Southwestern's transition to a liberal arts college at this time. Both administrations were independent of each other. Mr. Wilmot Dalferes, prominent SLI alumnus stated that neither school was concerned with competing academically. The close relationship between these schools may also be noted by the fact that President Stephens was an active member in the LSU Alumni Association.

In 1921 a new announcement of Southwestern Louisiana Institute of Liberal and Technical Learning appeared. As a tuition-free state institution of higher learning Southwestern offered four-year courses leading to the Bachelors of Arts and Sciences, Education, and Home Economics. These degrees provided the certificate holders with the eligibility to teach in Louisiana's high schools.

Two-year junior college courses at Southwestern included Teacher Training, Home Economics, pre-Medical, pre-Legal, pre-Agricultural, and pre-Engineering. These courses did not grant a Bachelor's degree. This was also true of the special vocational courses in Stenography, Commercial subjects, Agricultural subjects and Mechanic Arts.

The special high school department was discontinued after September 1923. As a school of liberal and technical learning, Southwestern's curriculum included programs in physical education, gymnastics, athletics and music.[4]

Louisiana residents unable to attend Southwestern regularly but who desired to study certain courses led to the development of Southwestern's Division of Extension under the directorship of Harry J. Stahl in 1922. Courses offered in this department included

> business administration, commerce, education, English, French, geography, history, journalism, psychology, physics, sociology and accounting.[5]

By 1928 extension centers were in Houma, Opelousas, Abbeville, Leesville, Lafayette, New Iberia, Crowley and

Ville Platte. A twelve-member faculty offered 23 courses; 110 courses were offered by correspondence with an enrollment of 643 students.[6] The rapid growth in enrollment in the Division of Extension resulting from a convenient educational facility reflects the desire for education which existed among southwest Louisiana residents during the twenties but was previously not attainable. The Division of Extension and its purpose may be compared to President Stephens's program of adult education during the early 1900s and may well have been an outgrowth of the same program.

A reorganization of the semester schedule made by the State Board of Education in 1923 provided that all Louisiana colleges under their supervision were to have trimesters of twelve-week duration, and a summer term of six weeks. A program began for holding two six-week summer sessions if the need presented itself.[7]

The president of Southwestern came under fire of local politicians several times during his thirty-eight year term. A debate in the fall of 1923 between Stephens and Fernand Mouton, member of the State Board of Education from Lafayette and former Lieutenant-Governor, developed from an accusation made by Mouton charging Stephens with irregularities in Southwestern's budget.[8] As a result of Mouton's accusations President Stephens openly asked for "the fullest hearing and searching inquiry..."[9] to determine the facts causing the dispute. The exact charges made by Mouton against Stephens were

> extravagance and irregular methods in the disbursement of state funds allotted to Southwestern Louisiana Institute under his direction and supervision for the maintenance and support of said institution,

also

> general mismanagement of the business affairs of the Southwestern Louisiana Institute by him and under his direction and Supervision as president and business manager.[10]

34

Stephens rebutted Mouton's charges by stating that all information concerning Southwestern's budget had been made available to Mouton. The State Board of Education found no such evidence as charged by Mouton and declared that Southwestern was in excellent condition[11] and Stephens was subsequently exonerated of all accusations.[12]

A further eruption of relations between President Stephens and Fernand Mouton developed in 1926. During a meeting of the State Board of Education, Stephens' request for a pay raise for Southwestern's registrar from $1800 to $3000 a year caused Mouton to ask the duties of Southwestern's registrar. This question displeased Stephens and an argument quickly developed. The argument during the meeting over the increase in salary resumed following the meeting, and Stephens and Mouton engaged in a physical duel. Dr. Glen Smith of Amite and member of the State Board of Education witnessed the scuffle. He stated:

I do not know whether that [the argument during the meeting] was the real cause or whether it was some personal feeling of long standing.[13]

The physical encounter and the description of the cause of the scuffle between Mouton and Stephens shows personal bitterness between these two men. Dismissing personality conflicts the faculty of Southwestern stood firmly behind Stephens describing him as an

able president and leader, a man of the highest character, a man actuated by the purest motives and high sense of honor.[14]

The student body stated that it held President Stephens in "highest esteem" and that it resented Mr. Mouton's "hostile attitude toward Southwestern."[15] This popularity of Stephens among faculty and student body helped him to remain as president of Southwestern for thirty-eight years.

After twenty-nine years of service Stephens' continuance as president came to a vote before the State Board of

Education. The student body and faculty of Southwestern, the Parent Teacher Association of Lafayette, and the Southwestern Alumni expressed their support for Stephens.[16] Again Stephens remained at Southwestern.

Perhaps a testimony of Stephens' competence derives from the fact that in 1924 his partisans around the state supported him for the presidency of Louisiana State University. Stephens' disinterested reply to his boosters in regard to his being named president was that the final decision requires

> serious consideration and means much to the future of the state and I am certain that it will be treated wisely and well. So let us let the matter rest there for the present.[17]

This statement would have been again applicable in 1926 when Stephens was once more considered as president for the State University in Baton Rouge. A newspaper article at this time described Stephens as

> a man fitted by preparation, by ability, and by experience to place our great State University in the foremost ranks of American educational institutions and to maintain its standing as a leader in the realms of erudition.[18]

President Stephens' educational leadership speaks for itself. In the fall of 1925 when Southwestern had been admitted to the Association of Southern Colleges and Secondary Schools of the South, he stated that Southwestern met the standards of American Colleges in the quality of its faculty, the value of its physical plant, and the development of its library and educational laboratories.[19] Stephens expressed thanks to all the people who made this achievement possible following five years of work. He recognized the fact that without this support it would not have been possible for Southwestern to be accepted by the Association.[20]

Admission to the Association of Southern Colleges and Secondary Schools required that Southwestern maintain an

Girard Hall, one of the first buildings on Southwestern's campus, was named in honor of a Southwest Louisiana family. Southwestern's original campus was a donation by Mrs. Maxim E. Girard and her son. Crow Girard.

Southwestern Archives

adequate library. Southwestern's library, then located in Martin Hall, contained approximately 900 volumes in 1916.[21] Private donations, the largest which was the Gustave Breaux Memorial Library Collection, provided Southwestern's library with rare items, such as L'Abbe Cyprien Tanguay's seven volume *Dictionnaire Genealogique des Familles Canadiennes*. The Breaux Collection was donated by Colonel Gustave Arvilien Breaux of Lafayette who was a Confederate soldier, jurist, and scholar. An annual gift of one hundred dollars to the library supplemented the donation. Mrs. Breaux continued the donations to Southwestern following Mr. Breaux's death in 1910.[22]

By 1924, Southwestern's library, now housed in Girard Hall, contained 8,000 volumes.[23] During this year, Miss Edith G. Dupré donated to Southwestern eighty-seven reference volumes from the library of her late brother, Congressman H. Garland Dupré.[24] Also during this year, Southwestern fulfilled the Southern Association's requirement by employing a professionally trained librarian, Miss Lois Shortess.[25]

The importance of the library and its function in educational training resulted in library courses being offered at Southwestern primarily for teachers who worked part-time in high school libraries.[26] By 1931 Southwestern could boast of having the second largest college library in the state next to LSU with a total of 15,000 volumes, which was continuously increasing in size.[27]

President Stephens was influential in spearheading practically all of Southwestern's educational accomplishments during his presidency. In appreciation for his friendliness and service to Southwestern, the graduating class of 1935 donated a portrait of him by Ellsworth Woodward to Southwestern.[28]

Stephens' accomplishments are summed up by Florence Kennedy:

Starting with twenty-five acres of land and one hundred forty-six students Southwestern Louisiana Institute under his direction gained recognition and rating among the state's most useful colleges, won educational prestige as an accredited member of the Southern Association of Colleges and Secondary Schools, and multiplied its student enrollment and acreage, which approached one thousand four hundred students and over a hundred acres of campus in the year of his retirement from its active leadership.[29]

In 1938 Stephens made an application for immediate retirement. At this time he had been President of Southwestern for thirty-eight years, and was now sixty-five years old. President Stephens delivered a resignation speech to the State Board of Education stating:

With the able and devoted assistance of my colleagues in Faculty and Staff, and with your constant encouragement, I feel that I have had a considerable degree of success in building and developing the institution into a standard college of high efficiency. It is so recognized and approved by both regional and national accrediting Associations.[30]

There was no political "connection" between Stephens' retirement and Lether Frazar's appointment as President of Southwestern.[31] Stephens was "of age to retire"[32] and left his office in Martin Hall "thirty-eight years to the minute, the hour, and the day"[33] from his appointment as Southwestern's first president. Upon resignation Stephens was made President Emeritus of Southwestern with an allowance of $4,000 a year,[34] as a gesture of appreciation for his accomplishments. President Stephens' guidance brought Southwestern's admission to the Southern Association of Colleges and Secondary Schools in 1925, the American Association of Colleges in 1926, the American Council on Education in 1927, and the Association of Colleges for Teacher Education in 1932. Southwestern also became a member of the American Association of Teachers Colleges with a "high rating" in 1932.[35]

Southwest Louisiana needed a college because of the historically underdeveloped educational facilities in the area.

President Stephens' enthusiastic leadership facilitated the development of the Institute into a full-fledged and accredited liberal arts college. Administrative problems cannot be overlooked; however, Stephen's determination overcame many of the barriers to Southwestern's continued growth. By the time President Stephens retired the Southwestern Louisiana Industrial Institute of Liberal and Technical Learning was contributing significantly to eliminating the educational poverty of both the young and the old in southwest Louisiana. It provided an opportunity of advancement to many young people of Louisiana to whom such opportunities had been previously lacking.

CHAPTER IV

THE FRAZAR ADMINISTRATION, 1938-40

Lether Edward Frazar's presidency at Southwestern might be described as an administration characterized by physical growth. Why such numerous construction projects? Louisiana politics is the answer. During the Frazar administration Louisiana politics was in a state of transition.

The Kingfish of Louisiana, Huey Pierce Long, was a byword to all Louisianians by the early 1930s. With his famous Share-Our-Wealth program Long became a national figure as a United States Senator in 1932.[1] Long was aggressive and soon became a rival to President Franklin Delano Roosevelt and the New Deal. As a result of political rivalry and Long's uninhibited tongue, Louisiana suffered. Long criticized the President's vacation cruising on millionaire Vincent Astor's yacht and dubbed Roosevelt as "Prince Franklin, Knight of the Nourmahal."[2] In retaliation for this derogatory remark, Roosevelt curtailed over $10,000,000 of the Public Works Administration (PWA) construction funds to Louisiana. Long's assassination in 1935 ended this.

When Frazar became president of Southwestern in 1938, Louisiana was granted its PWA funds. As Allan P. Sindler states in *Huey Long's Louisiana,* "scarcely had the Kingfish been interred" when in 1936 Longite Governor Richard W. Leche befriended the Roosevelt administration and Louisiana received its withheld PWA construction funds.[3] This enabled construction projects at Southwestern.

Lether Frazar became the second president of Southwestern Louisiana Institute on January 1, 1938. Frazar, born in DeRidder, Louisiana, on December 1, 1904, received his Bachelor of Arts degree in history from Southwestern in 1928 and his Master of Arts degree from Louisiana State University in 1932. He did post-graduate work at Columbia University in New York in 1941 and 1942. Prior to being chosen president of Southwestern, Frazar had served as principal of Longville, Jackson, and Merryville High Schools.[4]

41

Lether E. Frazar, Southwestern's second president, presiding at groundbreaking ceremonies in 1938 for the A. W. Bittle Student Center.

Southwestern Archives

During the years of 1932 to 1936 Frazar was not only a principal of several Louisiana high schools, but also became President of the Southwestern Graduate Club, an alumni organization, in 1933; a member of the Executive Council of the Louisiana Teachers' Association in 1935; and President of that organization in 1936. In 1936 Frazar was elected to the Louisiana State Legislature as the representative from Beauregard Parish.[5] It was then that President Frazar co-authored the present-day Teacher Retirement Law of Louisiana which established the Teachers' Retirement System and the Teachers' Retirement Fund used to provide income to retired school teachers.[6]

Frazar became president of Southwestern Louisiana Institute by unanimous appointment of the State Board of Education in 1938, and Edwin L. Stephens was simultaneously retired by the board.[7] Frazar was still a member of the Louisiana Legislature when he became president. There is no doubt that Frazar's political connection with the powerful Long faction of Louisiana aided his appointment; however, Frazar made no attempt to remove President Stephens from Southwestern.[8] As a result of Frazar's political affiliations, the editor of the Lafayette *Daily Advertiser* cautiously stated:

It is to be sincerely hoped that the course laid down by Dr. Stephens will be followed that nothing will happen that will take away from the young men and young women of Southwestern Louisiana the opportunity to secure a college education on an accredited basis that will prepare them to go forth into any part of the country with credits that will be accepted and have them as ready as possible to enter whatever walk of life that their plans may shape for them.[9]

President Frazar was a politician; however, while at Southwestern he was described by a member of the faculty as "primarily an educator concerned chiefly with Southwestern and its students."[10]

President Frazar's initial proposal for Southwestern's growth included new dormitories, physical education

Stephens Memorial Library was named in honor of Southwestern's first President—Edwin Lewis Stephens.

Southwestern Archives

facilities for women, a fine arts building, and a new library.[11] These proposals supplemented the two newly completed men's cooperative dormitories, and the new Atwood William Bittle Student Center.[12] Construction was begun immediately on the girl's dormitory (Thomas H. Harris Hall) and a new dining hall to accommodate the cooperative dormitories.[13] These buildings were only the beginning of the physical expansion program.

Shortly after President Frazar assumed office, he stated briefly his goals for Southwestern: "to build Southwestern Louisiana Institute into the greatest college in the South...."[14] The success of President Frazar's proposals for Southwestern's building program depended on ample financial appropriations. Frazar was able to obtain the necessary appropriations through his close friendship with State Superintendent of Education Thomas H. Harris and the Long forces in Louisiana during the late thirties.[15] Funds from the State Board of Education totaling $1,400,000 were supplemented in 1938 by $1,060,000 of Public Works Administration funds, equally apportioned to the institutions of higher learning in Louisiana.[16] These additional funds made President Frazar's physical development program more successful.[17] Frazar's objective of physical expansion was firmly established by the end of his first year as president. In fact, during the first year of his administration, three new buildings were completed and twelve others were begun, an expansion program representing over two million dollars.[18]

Two of the buildings were dedicated to pioneer educators of Southwestern. The Science Building (presently Broussard Hall) was named in honor of Southwestern's first president, Edwin Lewis Stephens.[19] The Academic Building (presently Mouton Hall)[20] was named in honor of Southwestern's first English instructor, Edith Garland Dupré.[21] The new infirmary was dedicated to Dr. Merrick Edmond Saucier, prominent physician and former member of the State Board of Education.[22] The dedication of the new library building (presently Edwin L. Stephens) and the new education training building (presently Fuller M. Hamilton)[23] also occurred during Frazar's presidency. The new elementary training school provided teacher training for students in the College of Education.

President Frazar soon realized the importance of an increase in enrollment. His efforts were directed at gaining more students from the immediate area. In order to promote this purpose, he enlarged the commuter bus system from Kaplan, Esterwood, New Iberia, Church Point, and St. Martinville to include Opelousas and the surrounding area. By so doing Frazar made Southwestern accessible to practically all potential students of the greater Lafayette area.[24]

President Frazar increased the faculty of Southwestern as the enrollment rose.[25] During his presidency, Frazar expanded the faculty from ninety to ninety-six members, and provided for sixteen teachers for the new Elementary Training School.[26] A larger faculty provided for a better teacher-student ratio, thus improving Southwestern's standard instruction.

Through Frazar's leadership Southwestern gained a Department of Music in 1938,[27] and developed further its Division of Extension. The Department of Extension had been organized in 1922 to provide educational instruction for potential students unable to attend regular courses.[28]

Southwestern added several new courses during Frazar's administration. Classes in veterinary science, truck and tractor maintenance, and creamery work were added to the agriculture courses,[29] and a visual education program was instituted.[30] Courses in airplane mechanics and pilot training,[31] dance,[32] and journalism[33] were also begun.

During the Frazar administration Southwestern created two new colleges, Agriculture and Engineering, by removing courses from the College of Liberal Arts.[34] Joel Lafayette Fletcher, professor of Agriculture, was named Dean of Agriculture[35] and George Griffin Hughes, professor of Engineering was named Dean of the College of Engineering.[36]

One of the commuter buses which brought students daily to Southwestern from the surrounding towns.
Southwestern Archives

Aware of Southwestern's educational growth and development, Thomas H. Harris, State Superintendent of Education, stated as early as 1939 that he would recommend to the State Board of Education that Southwestern be given a Graduate School.[37] This proposal, however, did not soon become a reality.

President Frazar's administration lasted only three years. President Frazar was appointed in 1939 by Governor Earl Kemp Long as Chairman of the Louisiana Highway Commission, a position which Frazar admittedly accepted because of the "absolute insistence" of Governor Long.[38] President Frazar was given a ninety-day leave,[39] but less than a week after the appointment he resigned and admitted that he realized he could be of little help to the people of Louisiana in such a short time. As a result of his appointment to the Highway Commission on the eve of the Louisiana scandals, Frazar was included in the accusation of irregularities and misconduct of the Commission's purchase of trucks used for highway construction. Frazar, however, was later exonerated of the charges by V. John Rogge, the official who investigated the case. Thus, President Frazar returned to Southwestern.[40]

Approximately a year after his temporary position as Chairman of the Louisiana Highway Commission, President Frazar resigned as President of Southwestern, probably as a result of the incoming anti-Long administration of Governor Sam Houston Jones. Frazar stated that his reason for resignation was "in the interest of Southwestern," and resulted in his desire "to give the new administration a free hand," a statement he made at the first meeting of the State Board of Education under the administration of Governor Sam Jones.[41]

President Frazar's resignation was voluntary[42] probably because he knew that he would have been fired by the anti-Long administration of Governor Jones even though Frazar and Jones were cousins.[43] It is doubtful whether Frazar could have remained president while Sam Jones's anti-Long reform administration governed Louisiana. It is a fact, however, that Frazar's administration while at Southwestern increased the physical plant, the enrollment, the faculty and the status of Southwestern in general.

After leaving Southwestern, Lether Frazar became Administrative Officer of the Office of Price Administration in Washington, D.C. He kept this position until 1942 when he became state director of the Louisiana Office of Price Administration. In 1944, Frazar joined the faculty of the John McNeese Junior College in Lake Charles, Louisiana, as Dean. He served in this capacity until 1950 when he became President of McNeese State College.[44] Frazar retained the office of President of McNeese up to his election as Lieutenant-Governor of the Earl Long administration 1956-1960.[45] Shortly after this term of office, Frazar died at the age of fifty-five on May 16, 1960, as a result of coronary illness.[46]

Although Lether Frazar remained but briefly as Southwestern's president, his objective "to build Southwestern..." provided necessary physical expansion. If Frazar's presidency were to be briefly described, it might properly be called "project expansion." Within three years, Frazar increased construction work on Southwestern's campus to over two million dollars as compared to $469,870 spent on major construction from 1901 to 1938.[47] During his presidency a total of twenty buildings was dedicated. This vast expansion program provided the "elbow room" necessary for the growth of Southwestern while simultaneously increasing Southwestern's educational potential.

49

Joel Lafayette Fletcher served as Southwestern's third president from 1941-1966.

Southwestern Archives

CHAPTER V

THE FLETCHER ADMINISTRATION, 1941-1966

During the years of the Fletcher administration, Southwestern's growth was the greatest in its history, both academically and physically. This chapter is a summary of the development and transition of Southwestern from a college of liberal and technical learning to a full-fledged university. Joel Lafayette Fletcher guided Southwestern through these years of growth and transition.

Joel L. Fletcher was born in Natchitoches, Louisiana, on January 12, 1897. His family moved to Colfax, Louisiana, in Grant Parish, and when Fletcher was eight years old the family moved to Lincoln Parish near Ruston, where the Fletcher children could receive a public education. In 1911, he entered Louisiana Industrial Institute (Louisiana Polytechnic University) in Ruston. Completing coursework at the Louisiana Industrial, Fletcher entered LSU in 1915 as a sophomore majoring in agriculture. From LSU he joined the Navy in 1918 for the duration of World War I. Upon completion of his service stint, Fletcher became assistant county agent of Union Parish, remaining there for only one year.[1]

While assistant county agent of Union Parish, Fletcher married Frances McLees, a childhood acquaintance, on October 15, 1919.[2]

Fletcher's career as an educator began in 1920, when he joined the faculty of Southwestern, widely known as "Dr. Stephens' School," as Assistant Professor of Agriculture on June 21, 1920.[3] In 1925 he resumed studies at Iowa State Agriculture and Mechanical College where he received a Master of Science degree in Agriculture in 1926. In this same year Fletcher returned to his position at Southwestern, and in 1938 he became the Dean of the newly organized College of Agriculture.[4]

Lether Frazar announced his retirement as President of Southwestern in 1940. Following this announcement the State Board of Education appointed a committee to study the possible candidates for president of Southwestern. Joel Lafayette Fletcher, Dean of the College of Agriculture and Harry Lewis Griffin, Dean of the College of Liberal Arts were the two leading candidates.[5] The special committee recommended Fletcher for the post, and in November, 1940, John E. Coxe, State Superintendent of Education announced Fletcher's appointment by a unanimous decision of the Board.[6]

Fletcher formally became President of the Southwestern Louisiana Institute on January 1, 1941. As he assumed office he stated:

I shall endeavor as president of Southwestern Louisiana Institute to insure the maintenance of the high standard of liberal and cultural education that has become a traditional part of this college, and to stress vocational education so that the boys and girls who leave Southwestern will be more efficiently prepared to do their life's work and to secure for themselves a place in society where they will become useful citizens.[7]

During his administration Fletcher was guided by the philosophy of the great educator, Edwin Anderson Alderman. Alderman was from North Carolina, served as President of Tulane, 1900-1904; and President of the University of Virginia, 1904-1931.[8] Like Alderman, President Fletcher believed, "Every human being has the same right to be educated as he has to be free."[9]

Educational training as once described by Fletcher is "the basic fundamental for survival today."[10] To emphasize the importance of educational training, Fletcher stated, "Property and money may be lost, but a child who acquires a thorough education will have that possession all of his life.[11]

President Fletcher supported financial aid to students to increase the opportunity for training at Southwestern in his farm-education program organization in 1936.[12] This he did to maintain his belief that "Every child who has the ambition for, and ability to achieve, a college education should be afforded an opportunity to do so."[13] This philosophy enabled an increase in enrollment through student aid projects.

Shortly after President Fletcher assumed office he made administrative changes. Thomas J. Arceneaux, Professor of Agriculture, was named Dean of the College of Agriculture; and Joseph A. Rhiel, Associate Professor of History, was named Dean of Men and also served as Dean of Liberal Arts, and Robert May came to Southwestern later and became Dean of Liberal Arts and Dean of Education, respectively. These devoted educators remained at Southwestern throughout the Fletcher administration. President Fletcher acknowledges Deans Frederick Zurburg, Herbert Hamilton, Agnes Edwards, and the late Maxime Doucet; and the late Mrs. Muriel McCulla Price, and Mary Dichmann of whom he says "played an important part in my administration."[14]

A new registration program, initiated in 1947, provided that enrolled students could meet their counselors to organize their curriculum schedules for the upcoming semester.[15] This new system provided that complete class-schedule cards were received by the students the first day of the new semester. By 1946 this pre-registration system was completed and partially ended long registration lines.[16] This new procedure made the registration of students more efficient.

The Southern Association of Colleges and Secondary Schools had placed Southwestern on probation in 1940 during Frazar's administration because there were too many students per instructor in the English and mathematics classes. The probation was removed, however, during Fletcher's first year as president when he acted vigorously to remedy the deficiencies.[17]

During the early years of the Fletcher administration Southwestern played an important role in training programs in World War II. The United States Office of Education allotted $32,968 to Southwestern in 1941 for purchasing equipment to train national defense workers. Training in mechanics, welding, machine shop, electrical, sheet metal,

A representative from the United States Navy presented a plaque to Southwestern as a result of the efficiency of the V-12 Program on the campus during World War II. Receiving the plaque is Thomas J. Arceneaux, Dean of Agriculture.

Southwestern Archives

aircraft blueprinting, reading, and sketching constituted the program.[18] This was only one phase of Southwestern's participation in national defense.

In 1934 Southwestern became designated by the United States Navy as a Navy College Training Center. The men in this V-12 program were "on active duty with base pay, subsistence, uniforms, medical care and tuition."[19] Courses offered in a basic and premedical curriculum included mathematics, English, history, chemistry, physics, foreign language, and physical training. As a result of the Navy training program Southwestern operated on a year-round basis consisting of three terms lasting sixteen weeks each. This arrangement continued through the 1945-46 school year.[20]

President Fletcher's office prepared newsletters to the students of SLI who were serving their country. These letters provided information of Southwestern's activities and were important in keeping a close relationship between the students and Southwestern.[21] Many of these student-servicemen returned to Southwestern after the war to complete their education.

Following World War II Southwestern discontinued its Navy V-12 program which had become an important part of campus activity during the war.[22] As a result of the efficiency of the V-12 program at Southwestern, a certificate was given to the Institute by the Navy. Representatives from all states except Rhode Island, Vermont and Delaware participated in the program on Southwestern's campus. Servicemen from Mexico, Puerto Rico, Washington, DC and Hawaii were also represented. The certificate awarded to Southwestern stated:

This mark of commendation is awarded to the Navy Department of Southwestern Louisiana Institute for effective cooperation with the United States Navy in the training of officer candidates under the Navy V-12 program from July 1, 1943, until October 31, 1945.[23]

The veteran enrollment at Southwestern increased as the soldiers returned home from the war. The veterans of

An unidentified Veteran and Dr. Joel L. Fletcher (President of Southwestern, 1941-1966) stand before a Memorial Plaque erected by the Veteran's Club of SLI in 1950.

Southwestern Archives

THE FLETCHER ADMINISTRATION

Southwestern organized a Veteran's Club for "better relations with the other students for the betterment of all concerned."[24] The 1947 enrollment of veterans was 1,700 or 60% of the student body. To provide for this large percentage of veteran students, apartments sprouted on the campus and also the nearby Lafayette Municipal Airport. These included 200 apartments on campus and 50 at the airport. The veterans and their activities were under the administration of Col. W. L. Bruner.[25] By 1949, however, the veteran enrollment dropped to 1,000 or 40% of the enrollment.[26]

As a result of the increase in men students, the physical education department was reorganized in 1945 to meet the post-war demand. The department expanded to provide for the opportunity that every interested student might major in physical education, and also to provide an opportunity for every student to enjoy a thorough physical fitness program. Robert L. Browne became the head of the newly organized department.[27]

The post-war increase of students at Southwestern brought its enrollment to 3,243, which was the largest of Louisiana's colleges. Southwestern's enrollment surpassed the combined enrollment of Louisiana Polytechnic Institute and Southeastern Louisiana College (Southeastern Louisiana University) in 1946.[28]

The drop in freshman enrollment occurred in the 1949-50 session at Southwestern because of the change made by the Department of Education which required a twelve-year high school program instead of the usual eleven-year program. The total enrollment in 1948 was 3,370 and the 1949 enrollment dropped to 2,883.[29]

The decrease did not harm Southwestern academically. In one instance, for example, the National Association of Schools of Music accredited Southwestern's music department in 1950 as a result of the high standards of the department.[30]

Increased construction of academic buildings occurred following World War II. In naming the new buildings and streets on the campus, former faculty members' names were usually honored. In 1950 streets began to be named in honor of past faculty members. Hebrard Boulevard was named for Miss Gabrielle Hebrard, professor of French at SLI for nearly a quarter of a century, 1913-37. Woodson Street was named for Ashby Woodson, former head of the department of engineering, 1901-29. Boucher Street was named for Alice N. Boucher, supervising critic teacher at Hamilton Training School for many years.[31]

Physical expansion went hand-in-hand with academic expansion. The College of Nursing was organized at Southwestern in 1951

to prepare nurses who meet high standards of nursing practice with confidence and with personal satisfaction while rendering the maximum benefit to the patient.[32]

Southwestern thus had the only College of Nursing of the institutions under the State Board of Education. The other institutions, however, did have schools and departments of nursing.[33] The nursing curriculum at Southwestern consisted of two academic years at the college and the remaining time gaining practical experience and education from affiliated hospitals and nursing organizations.[34]

In 1952 the College of Commerce was organized at Southwestern by separating the Department of Economics and Business from the College of Liberal Arts.[35] The new College consisted of the departments of Accounting, Business Administration, Economics, and Secretarial Science.[36]

Another change in the academic administrative system was made in 1953. The home economics department was converted to the School of Home Economics at Southwestern. Miss Marie Louise Comeaux became director. This new school provided a facility for the increasing enrollment in home economics.[37] These academic expansions brought Southwestern closer to its transition to a university.

The physical growth of Southwestern in 1953 produced a need for a new $25,000 telephone exchange on the campus.[38] The new PBX replaced the individual telephones

Freshman registration in 1926 resulted in long lines in front of Old Martin Hall.

Southwestern Archives

on campus and provided for a more efficient intra-campus communication system. Another technological improvement on Southwestern's campus made in 1954 was the "electronic brain" or computer. The computer was first used in a mathematics course taken by senior science and engineering students. The machine, used primarily for instructional purposes, was available to business and industry of southwest Louisiana.[39] By the summer of 1960 Southwestern used the computer in the registration of its students. This new method of "computer" registration made the process more rapid and efficient.[40]

Technological change was not the sole change of the early '50s. Prior to 1954 only white students were eligible to enter Southwestern. On January 8, 1954, four Lafayette Negroes: Clara Dell Constantine, Martha Jane Conway, Charles Vincent Singleton and Shirley Taylor filed suit to have the Shreveport federal court end Southwestern's policy of racial segregation. Named as defendants were Joel L. Fletcher, president; James Stewart Bonnet, registrar; Mrs. Eleanor H. Meade, immediate past president of the State Board of Education; the Board of Education and board members individually. The plaintiffs charged that Southwestern was violating the Fourteenth Amendment by not admitting Negroes through the "denial of property without due process of law."[41]

In February of the same year the plaintiff's contention was summarized as follows:

> It would be a hardship for the Lafayette residents to travel to Southern University at Scotlandville near Baton Rouge, a state supported negro school.[42]

On April 23, Federal Judges Wayne G. Borah, Edwin F. Hunter and Ben C. Dawkins ordered Southwestern to admit Negroes because of a lack of equal accommodations in southwest Louisiana for Negro education. President Fletcher responded to the court ruling:

> It's our policy to make no comment on such things. The ruling was directed to the state board of education, I understand.[43]

President Fletcher's response of "no comment" is characteristic of all proceedings relating to Southwestern's integration by the administration.

Approximately a week after the court's ruling that no equal education facilities existed for the Negro in southwest Louisiana, a resolution offered by George Madison passed the Legal Committee of the State Board of Education authorizing an appeal to the United States Supreme Court.[44] The Supreme Court was at that time reviewing segregation in the Southern states. On May 17, the Supreme Court's ruling on segregation (*Brown v. Board of Education*, 347 U.S. 483) made Southwestern's attempt to maintain segregation futile. Chief Justice Earl Warren speaking for the Supreme Court stated in a court decision on segregation that:

> We conclude that in the field of public education the doctrine of separate but equal...has no place. Separate educational facilities are inherently unequal.[45]

Several days later the Supreme Court broadened its decision "with Orders designed to admit Negroes to publicly supported colleges, universities, theaters, golf courses, and housing projects."[46]

In June 1954, a Negro woman attempted to register on the federal court case ruling. Registration was denied her by the Registrar, J. Stewart Bonnet, who stated that he could not register her without the State Board of Education's authorization.[47]

On July 18, 1954, the Shreveport Federal Court gave a final judgment on the case presented before it in January of that year.

> The judgment decreed that the board of Education, the SLI president, registrar, and their successors be permanently enjoined from refusing to admit any Negro to the school because of race or color.[48]

Subsequently, the first Negro, John Harold Taylor, of Arnaudville, Louisiana, registered in the College of

Engineering on July 22, 1954, alone and without incident. Thus, Southwestern became the first institution under the State Board of Education to be racially integrated.[49] Seventy-five Negro students registered at Southwestern for the 1954-55 session,[50] and by 1960, 205 Negroes were registered at Southwestern.[51]

In the spring of 1955 the Committee on Medical Education and Hospitals approved SLI for medical technology study at Lafayette Charity Hospital. Prior to this acceptance of the Committee, Southwestern's students finished their course work in medical technology in hospitals in Baton Rouge, Alexandria, New Orleans and Shreveport. This medical technology school made it easier for Southwestern's students in that the complete course could be studied while the student was at Southwestern.[52]

The Southwestern Louisiana Institute Foundation, organized in 1955 as a non-profit corporation, promoted Southwestern's material welfare. The major purpose of the Foundation was to provide supplementary funds to the state appropriations for academic and related activities at Southwestern. Fred W. Bates, Lafayette Foundation President, announced the first gift to the Foundation, $5,000 from Senator and Mrs. Eloi M. Girard in October, 1955.[53] Fifty-five years earlier the same family had donated the land which was Southwestern's original campus.

Southwestern's library facilities also expanded during President Fletcher's administration. Harry Smedes, one-time Southwestern student from Cade, donated a 200 book collection to the library in 1948. Some of the books in the collection were unobtainable, rare books.[54] The Caffery family library was donated to Southwestern by Ambassador Jefferson Caffery and his sister, Bessie Caffery, in memory of their father, the late Charles D. Caffery in 1949. The library consisted of writings of Thomas Jefferson, and the works entitled, "The World's Great Classics."[55]

By 1956 Stephens Memorial Library contained 110,000 volumes, not including government publications, unbound periodicals, and pamphlets. The annual receipt of 700

Blackham Coliseum, named in honor of Stafford M. Blackham, is the site of Southwestern's home basketball games as well as several civic activities.

Southwestern Archives

Randolph Hall was named for Beverly Randolph Stephens, eldest of President Edwin L. Stephens three daughters.

Southwestern Archives

periodicals and 5,000 books[56] provided students with necessary library material. In 1957, Southwestern's book stock was larger than any of the other Louisiana state colleges.[57] Southwestern's library grew continuously in volume gradually overcrowding the facilities of the existing library. By 1959 Stephens Memorial Library had increased in volume to 140,000 volumes and 880 periodicals[58] maintaining Southwestern's lead in library facilities among Louisiana's state colleges.

President Fletcher's administration provided for an expansion program on Southwestern's campus in fulfilling the needs of the increase in enrollment. Following World War II the first project of expansion was 100 housing units for the accommodation of married students, most of whom were veterans. In 1948 construction was completed on a plant for the instruction and practice in the manufacture of dairy products.

Southwestern's growth produced a need for a coliseum to seat large numbers of people. In 1949 the Blackham Coliseum[59] was dedicated for the use of livestock shows, basketball games and civic exhibitions. In 1950 three new girls' dormitories were constructed on Southwestern's campus. These were Baker, Huger, and Randolph Halls, and were named for past members of Southwestern's faculty.[60]

A new chemistry building was completed on the campus in 1952. Montgomery Hall[61] consisted of classrooms and laboratories used for instruction in science courses.

The Acadian heritage of southwest Louisiana is centered in the Lafayette area. In 1955 Southwestern acquired *La Maison Acadienne Française* for $50,500 from the heirs of Mrs. M. Meyers, formerly Louise Bendel. The use of the French House is for "the edification of the French Language and Acadien [sic] culture." Dr. Thomas Arceneaux, Dean of the College of Agriculture, and chairman for acquiring the cultural hall stated at the dedication that the purpose of the House was "an excellent center for the perpetuation of the French language and Acadian culture in this area."[62]

Montgomery Hall, named for William A. Montgomery, is the Chemistry Building and was completed in 1952.
Southwestern Archives

Charles D. Caffery, Rexford C. McCullogh, and J. Arthur Roy Halls are dormitories for men students at Southwestern. Southwestern Archives

La Maison Acadienne Francaise (The French House) was acquired in 1955 to help in perpetuating the French language in Southwest Louisiana.

Southwestern Archives

Campus-wide expansion began in 1956. The construction of Roy and Caffery[63] dormitories for men, and the Student Union Buildings increased living and recreation areas for Southwestern's students. The main building of the three building Student Center complex was the Memorial Student Center named Guillory Hall. Coronna and Olivier Halls were the bookstore and office building, and the men and women's clubrooms respectively.[64] These buildings were evidence of Southwestern's growth.

In 1957 Southwestern's physical facilities were further expanded with the construction of a modern dairy, the Resweber Building; engineering building, Madison Hall; and biological sciences building, Billeaud Hall.[65]

In 1959 renovations were made to Brown Ayers Hall and O. K. Allen Dining hall. Twenty additional apartments were constructed on campus for married students.[66] These constructions on the campus enlarged the physical plant and simultaneously provided faculty and students with a more pleasant educational environment.

Not only physical expansion, but academic progress is characteristic of President Fletcher's administration. A brief summary of Southwestern's scholastic requirements is in order. The scholastic regulations at Southwestern were vaguely stated in the school catalog up to the 1929-30 session. From 1929-33 freshmen students were required to earn at least nine quarter hours per quarter, and sophomores, juniors, and seniors were required to earn twelve. By 1942 students were regulated by cumulative average determined on a graduated scale with a 1.0 average on a 3.0 system for good standing[67] following eight semesters of course work. By the 1959-60 session scholastic requirements stated in the catalog changed the good standing standard to include that persons with six semester hours maintain a 1.0 average on a 3.0 system.[68]

By 1960 Southwestern consisted of eight separate colleges, each consisting of several departments. The College of Agriculture was departmentalized into home economics, agricultural engineering, animal husbandry, general agriculture,

Completed in 1957, H. Flood Madison Hall is the name given the engineering building complex on campus. Madison was once president of the Louisiana State Board of Education.

Southwestern Archives

Billeaud Hall is the biology building on campus and was named in honor of a southwest Louisiana family.

Southwestern Archives

plant industry, and vocational agricultural education. The departments of accounting, business administration, economics, finance, general business, management, marketing, and secretarial science made up the College of Commerce. The College of Engineering consisted of departments in chemical, civil, electrical, general business, geology, mechanical and petroleum engineering. The College of Education had as its departments audio visual, administration and techniques of teaching, education, geography and geology, health and physical education for men, health and physical education for women, music, psychology, and special education. Departments of air science, art and architecture, bacteriology, biology, chemistry, English, foreign languages, mathematics, music, physics, social studies, and speech made up the College of Liberal Arts. The Colleges of Nursing, Night and Special Division, and Graduate School were not departmentalized.[69]

Southwestern's grading system was on a three-point system in 1960. An 'A' equaled 3 quality points, a 'B' equaled 2 quality points, and a 'C' equaled 1 quality point.[70] This grading system had been used since Southwestern's early years, but was later changed to a four-point system.

State Superintendent of Education, Shelby M. Jackson wrote to President Fletcher in October 1956 announcing the State Board of Education's approval to providing Southwestern with a graduate school program.[71] This was a signal advancement for Southwestern's academic program. The National Council for Accreditation of Teacher Education accredited Southwestern in 1954, and the Engineers Council for Professional Development in 1955.[72]

Southwestern's graduate program introduced a new era to SLI's educational program. Southwestern's graduate school offered courses only in Education when it was first organized. The purposes of the graduate school were:

(1) to add the educational competence of teachers and other professional personnel involved in elementary and secondary education,

(2) to conduct studies and research in learning and

teaching at the elementary and secondary levels, and (3) to furnish field services to the schools of Louisiana.[73]

Southwestern's graduate school had 116 students for its first term, fall 1957. Of these 116, 18 were full time, and 98 were part time.[74] In December of 1957 Southwestern announced the inclusion of graduate study in three new fields: engineering, science, and mathematics.[75]

By 1958 the enrollment of Southwestern was 5,650 students. Of this total 5,156 were undergraduates, 127 were graduate students, and the night school and special division had an enrollment of 367.[76] During the 1959-60 school session, an increase in the faculty of thirty-two members boosted Southwestern's faculty to a total of 507 members.[77] This increase in faculty gave Southwestern a teacher-student ratio of 10.4 to 1.

By 1960 Southwestern's academic stature was established. In this year Senator Elmore Bonin of St. Martinville introduced a bill in the state to make Southwestern a university. Senator Sam Broussard of New Iberia, and Representatives Richard Bertrand and Louis Michot were also instrumental in the passage of the bill.[78]

Southwestern Louisiana Institute formally became the University of Southwestern Louisiana on July 27, 1960, when the bill became law.[79] Shortly after this a newspaper boastfully entitled its article, "From Today On, It'll Be Known as USL."

In response to Southwestern becoming a University, President Fletcher stated:

With the advent of this change in name and status, denoting as it does added prestige and dignity in the family of colleges and universities, come new responsibilities and challenges. As it has in the past, Southwestern will summon its strength to meet them... as we enter this new era of Southwestern's life of service to its community, state and nation, we re-dedicated ourselves to the high ideals of its founders and search for our added competence in the new and expanded fields of higher education.[80]

Joel Lafayette Fletcher's administration witnessed a rapid growth of Southwestern from 1941 to 1966. An increase in student enrollment and faculty made Southwestern a more important institution of learning to southwest Louisiana. By 1960 Southwestern had been accredited in fields of importance such as teacher education, agriculture, engineering, and music. The organization of two new colleges, nursing and commerce, also mark the academic growth experienced by Southwestern.

The Fletcher administration represents the later years of a process of steady educational development at Southwestern. The organization of the graduate school at USL may easily be compared and contrasted to the years when the Industrial Institute merely offered a high school education. From industrial high school, to liberal arts college, to post-graduate course work, to a university; Southwestern's educational standards developed on a steady but continuous incline. Building on a history of "loftiness of aspiration, honesty of purpose and generosity of comradeship"[81] Southwestern prepared for a propitious future.

The accomplishments of Joel L. Fletcher's administration may be condensed by stating that during the years 1941-1960 Southwestern built its educational base by profiting from previous shortcomings as ample physical facilities and a qualified faculty in preparation for the future. All was not accomplished. The educational hazards of academic expansion presented new problems. Expenses were greater. The difficulties in maintenance of adequate faculty and physical facilities expanded. Possibly, Southwestern could have become a stronger educational institution with a larger faculty and a more expansive academic curriculum without the problems which accompanied its growth. The increase in enrollment and the organization of a graduate school during the Fletcher administration, however, exemplify continuation of growth in building for a brighter future.

A summary of Southwestern's history is no easy chore. From its beginning as Industrial Institute which was in fact no more than a high school, Southwestern's administrative leadership gradually overcame problems of academic and physical expansion. Dr. Edwin L. Stephens continually strived to remove Southwestern's image of a "Lafayette High School." Attracting students from southwest Louisiana to attend the Industrial Institute, however, took second place to efforts to achieve academic excellence. In 1921, Dr. Stephens' determined efforts were realized in a new academic status for Southwestern as the Southwestern Louisiana Institute of Liberal and Technical Learning.

As a liberal arts college Southwestern faced even greater challenges. Through the years an experienced administration helped to decrease the problems which accompany academic growth. Physical growth at Southwestern was greatly facilitated by Dr. Lether Frazar during the years 1938-1940. Following Frazar's brief transitional administration, Joel L. Fletcher became Southwestern's president. This chapter has been an account of the Fletcher administration which is particularly vital because in these years Southwestern achieved the status of a full-fledged university. Southwestern's transition from an industrial institute to a liberal arts college (1921) into a full-fledged university (1960) can be attributed heavily to the strong academic foundations laid by Edwin Lewis Stephens between 1900 and 1938, the physical growth sponsored by Lether Frazar before World War II, and the solid academic development of the Fletcher administration as well as to the support of area citizens and dedicated faculty. Just as no person can live without nourishment, no respectable university can exist without the continuous upgrading of its present academic structure.

CHAPTER VI

ATHLETICS

The story of Southwestern's athletic program is an integral part of the growth of the institution from an industrial institute (1900-1921) to its conversion into a four-year liberal arts college (1921), and finally to a university (1960). Athletic activities have always played an important role in its program because of their appeal to the students and to the people of the area. Athletics makes both the students and patrons of Southwestern more aware of its educational and recreational purposes.

Southwestern's first athletic involvement with area schools was in the Interscholastic Athletic and Oratorical Association contest held on the campus in 1906. The Association, organized in 1904, created an athletic program which included most of the schools of southwest Louisiana. Representatives from New Iberia, Crowley, Lake Charles, Leesville, Marksville, St. Martinville, Breaux Bridge and Franklin High Schools as well as from Southwestern participated in the 1906 IAOA Rally.[1] The athletic events included the 100 yard dash, the 220 yard dash, 880 yard run, 440 yard run, 120 yard hurdles, 220 yard hurdles, mile run, the discus throw, pole vault, broad jump, shot put and the relay race.[2]

As early as 1907 a newspaper article described Southwestern's IAOA Rally as "the most important school event of the year in this section of the State."[3] It remained so for many years.

Although the University no longer actively participates, Southwestern continues to sponsor the IAOA Rally for the high schools from southwest Louisiana. Many schools have been added to the list of original participants which includes practically all high schools of the southwest Louisiana area and many from throughout the state. By 1928, 150 area schools were invited, and by the late fifties the 396 schools in the Louisiana High School Athletic Association were eligible to participate.[4]

The Red Jacket Club was organized in 1937 to boost Southwestern's athletic activities.

Southwestern Archives

Athletic booster organizations are important to the function of a prosperous athletic program. The Southwestern Louisiana Industrial Institute Athletic Association was formed in 1909 by the students and faculty

> to promote enthusiasm among the students and to unite in one organization the different branches of athletics in which the Institute participates....[5]

Several athletic "booster" organizations have sprouted on Southwestern's campus. The "S" Club was organized on May 28, 1922, "to help the cause of Athletics at the old school and to keep the old 'gang' together."[6] In 1927, the Southwestern Side-Lines Club was organized by enthusiastic supporters of the athletic teams. W. B. Vennard, first chairman of the Club, expressed its purpose as a "go between" between the public and Southwestern's athletic activities.[7]

The "Red Jacket Club," a women's organization intended to pep Southwestern's athletic activities, was organized in 1937. One of its major functions was the sale of season tickets.[8] Another similar organization, the Southwestern Boosters' Club, was organized in 1940 to initiate a similar program for the sale of season tickets. It was supported by the American Legion, Young Men's Business Club, Lions Club, Rotary Club and the Chamber of Commerce of Lafayette.[9]

Southwestern's athletic program has always attempted to supplement educational training with physical education. In the formative years the athletes had to meet scholastic requirements to participate in Southwestern's athletic program. In 1920, 12 hours of passing work per week was the minimum required for students to participate actively. During the fifties academic requirements for athletes were the same as for other students. Freshmen and sophomores were required to pass 6 semester hours, and juniors and seniors 9 semester hours per semester to remain enrolled as a student.[10]

The Lafayette *Daily Advertiser* has consistently backed Southwestern's athletic activity which it soon described as a "credit to the institution." Lafayette benefitted from a close relationship between its citizens and Southwestern's athletic program. This close bond is evident in the following editorial statement:

Southwestern Louisiana Institute is Lafayette. Pull for Southwestern. Its development in every phase means not only the development of a great Louisiana Educational institution, but it means a greater development for Lafayette. [11]

In 1925 a Survey Commission headed by Dr. W. C. Bagley, and Dr. Thomas Alexander of Columbia University studied the emphasis on athletic activity in Louisiana and described a "tendency to overemphasize athletics,..." at Southwestern. It concluded that as a result of the overemphasis "educational values are seriously marred." These findings were a criticism of Southwestern and the town of Lafayette for "going 'wild' over the result of a game."[12] Reference was subsequently made to the findings of the Survey commission. One newspaper observed,

praise be, for it shows that the town and the students are working hand in hand and heart to heart.[13]

Athletic functions have always been important to Southwestern and Acadiana. Jefferson Caffery, former student and coach, and then *Charge d'Affaires* for the United States' Embassy in Japan donated $200 to the Southwestern Louisiana Institute Athletic Association in 1923.[14] This donation sparked a drive by President Stephens, the faculty, the alumni, and the student body for funds to build a stadium under the chairmanship of the late Maurice Heymann. In 1925 in only three hours $37,690 was collected, and plans were made for the completion of the stadium by the end of 1926.[15] Heymann stated during the drive that

79

McNaspy Stadium, named for Clement J. McNaspy " Father of Athletics at Southwestern," at the 1947 Homecoming game.

Southwestern Archives

Every little MONOHIPPIC COLLEGE in the United States has a STADIUM. But a great TEN THOUSAND HORSEPOWER institution like SOUTHWESTERN has none.[16]

The Stadium complex plans included

a quarter-mile oval, with straightway, baseball diamond, football field, a good fence, five thousand seats, a swimming pool and a pavilion gymnasium with floor space for eighty feet by one hundred twenty feet – all at an expenditure of nearly $30,000.[17]

The dedication of the new stadium took place on October 15, 1926, for the Southwestern-Sam Houston Normal game. The grandstand seated 1,200 persons; 1,500 more were accommodated by a bleacher.[18] The stadium was named in 1940 in honor of Clement J. McNaspy, "Father of Athletics at Southwestern." McNaspy had come to Southwestern in 1909 and had been an outstanding athletic figure. He was praised during the naming of the stadium as

a man who stood for the highest development of amateur athletics, a development that meant character building and the finest type of sportsmanship.[19]

In 1924 the administration, faculty, and the students expressed an interest in becoming affiliated with the Southern Intercollegiate Athletic Association "to obtain wider recognition as a standard college in all respects...." This organization, similar to the Southland Conference of which Southwestern was to later become a member, accepted the institution in the spring of 1925.[20]

The recruiting of potential athletic standouts became a necessity for Southwestern to remain in competition with SIAA opponents. In 1937 scholarships were provided to attract outstanding athletes. An allotment of $10,500 in scholarships was provided for tuition fees, books, laundry, and room and board for prospective athletes.[21]

The Earl K. Long Gymnasium, dedicated in 1939, is better known as the Men's Gym.

Southwestern Archives

ATHLETICS

Southwestern's athletic complex grew rapidly after its admission to SIAA. In 1938 contract plans for a $154,000 gymnasium was to provide needed basketball courts, dressing rooms, classrooms, and offices for athletic officials.[22] The dedication of the Earl K. Long Gymnasium, held in January, 1939, included a program and a dance for the whole student body.[23]

In 1948 Southwestern became a member of the newly organized Gulf States Conference[24] which grew out of the SIAA.[25] During its first year of competition in the GSC Southwestern tied for second place with Louisiana Tech in overall competition.[26]

Football

Southwestern's football history is unique in comparison to colleges that have only participated in intercollegiate competition. Prior to 1921 Southwestern was still an industrial high school, and its athletic opponents included some of the area high schools such as Lake Charles, Crowley, and Broussard.[27] In 1908, the roster of the Industrial's opponents included St. Martinville, Crowley, New Iberia, Jennings, and Lake Charles High Schools.[28]

During Southwestern's athletic participation with area high schools transportation expenses to football games played with distant opponents were financed through gate receipts. Plans were also made for a most convenient and profitable location. Agreements were made between the managers of the opposing teams prior to the opening of the season, most of which were similar to the following between Louisiana Industrial Institute (Ruston) and Southwestern:

We are arranging our 1912 football schedule, and wish to play you at Alexandria, Thanksgiving, 1912, share equally expenses or profits.[29]

Sometimes the amount collected as gate receipts was not sufficient to pay all of the expenses. A letter from Southwestern's business office to Baton Rouge High School

The Foot Ball Team of 1903

Southwestern's Football Team of 1903.

Southwestern Archives

in 1909 explained the small amount of potential spectators in Lafayette, possibly the result of a poor record:

Lafayette is not a good football town and we could be unable to meet the expense of your team coming over here and returning.[30]

In 1916, however, Southwestern had a very successful football season gaining 239 points to her opponents 6. Her winning streak held for 1917 when she gained 336 points to her opponents' 26.[31] The athletic accomplishment encouraged athletic support and pride.

As Southwestern grew in enrollment and educational stature, she no longer participated in athletic contests with area high schools. By 1918 Southwestern's football opponents included St. Charles College (Grand Coteau), Louisiana State University (Baton Rouge), LSU Reserves (Baton Rouge), Louisiana College (Pineville), Springhill College (Springhill, Alabama), Jefferson College (Convent), Louisiana Industrial Institute (Ruston), Camp Beauregard (Beauregard Parish), and Louisiana State Normal (Natchitoches).[32] In 1923 Tulane (New Orleans), and Centenary (Shreveport) were included on the roster of SLI's football opponents.[33] This was quite a roster for this date.

Southwestern dropped Tulane and LSU in 1921 from its football roster because of the many defeats suffered at the hands of these two powerful teams.[34] Southwestern's roster still does not regularly include these teams.

In 1931 the first night football game at Lafayette was played between SLI and the Crockett Aviators from Fort Crockett, Texas. The newly installed illumination consisted of

giant flood lights, special transformers, and ten poles 65 feet high which...(were) used to suspend the large reflectors to permit perfect visibility from any angle on the sidelines.[35]

In 1938 Southwestern received national recognition. In this year Southwestern sported a record of 6 straight victories scoring 94 points to her opponents' 7. During this season Southwestern had won the Little Four Conference, described by a Southwestern student reporter as "the hottest little ivy league in the nation," defeating the other three Louisiana teams – Louisiana Normal (Northwestern State University), Louisiana Tech, and Louisiana College. This accomplishment marked Southwestern's best football record up to that date.[36] Southwestern's bright football victories during this year were partly a result of the brilliant playing of Glynn Abel. Abel was named to the All SIAA team, mentioned for honors on the Associated Press's Little America, and won honorable mention by the All America Advisory Board in *Colliers Magazine*.[37]

Several Louisiana colleges – Centenary, Louisiana Tech, Louisiana College and Southwestern – joined together in 1939 to form the Louisiana Intercollegiate Conference which included joint participation in the sports of football, track, tennis, and basketball.[38]

In the first year of the LIC, Southwestern won the Conference Championship by defeating Louisiana Normal in the play-offs.[39] In 1944 Southeastern Louisiana College was admitted as a member of the LIC increasing the number of participating colleges to six.[40]

Southwestern participated in the first Oil Bowl Activities in Houston, Texas, in 1944. The program read SLI versus Arkansas Agricultural and Mechanical with a prediction of SLI, 24 and A&M, 7.[41] Southwestern was victorious in its first bowl bid.

Baseball

Baseball, another of Southwestern's main sports, was organized in 1914. It was never, however, as enthusiastically supported as football. In 1914, the fans of Southwestern's baseball team, as well as the people of Lafayette became excited about the game between SLII and the Cincinnati Reds. Though this game was not an ordinary baseball match, it did provide wholesome athletic competition. The fact that the

The Southwestern Girl's Basketball Team in 1912.

Southwestern Archives

The Southwestern Basketball Team of 1913.

Southwestern Archives

Cincinnati Reds was a professional team made the 13-1 defeat more acceptable to Southwestern's fans. Another game between Southwestern and the Reds held in 1915 produced a similar result.[42]

In 1927 Southwestern gave up baseball because of a lack of interest and money. Football, track, golf, and tennis were retained on the roster of sports.[43] The intercollegiate baseball activities were resumed in 1939 after a twelve year lapse, and the baseball schedule for 1940 included the teams of the University of Iowa, Northwestern, Louisiana College, LSU, Louisiana Tech, University of Mississippi, Millsaps and Centenary. A twenty-two game slate marked the resumption of baseball activity for SLI.[44] By 1960 Southwestern's baseball opponents had included such teams as Sam Houston College, Loyola (New Orleans), Southern Illinois University, and Northern Illinois.[45]

Basketball

Southwestern began playing basketball as a school sport in 1912 and at first played area high schools, just as in football, then went on to play other colleges.[46] Through the years basketball has developed into an important and enthusiastically supported sport at Southwestern. By 1960 its basketball schedule included such schools as Lamar Tech, Loyola (New Orleans) New Mexico University, Springhill, Centenary, Southeastern, Northeastern, McNeese, Northwestern, Louisiana Tech and Louisiana College.[47]

Boxing

Boxing became a school sport in 1930 under the direction of Ed "Happy" Davis.[48] The sport became popular among the students and the people of Lafayette. In 1939 a crowd of 5,200 watched as SLI matched LSU.[49] The boxing schedule by 1940 included the University of Mississippi, Loyola (New Orleans), LSU, Louisiana Tech, the University of Florida and Miami University.[50]

Southwestern's boxing squad held a bright record in 1941. In fact, in that year, Southwestern placed second to the

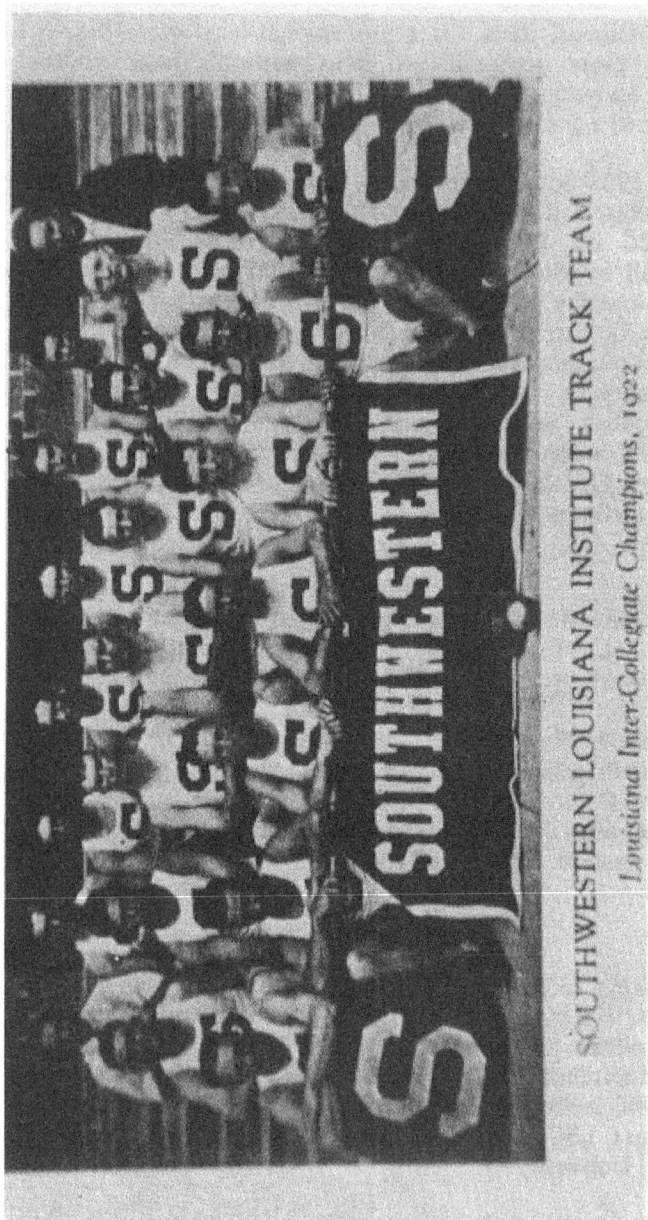

SOUTHWESTERN LOUISIANA INSTITUTE TRACK TEAM
Louisiana Inter-Collegiate Champions, 1922

The Southwestern Louisiana Institute Track Team, Louisiana Inter-Collegiate Champions, in 1922.
Southwestern Archives

University of Idaho in the National Collegiate Boxing Tournament held at the University of Pennsylvania. Although SLI had a strong boxing team, the sport was discontinued after 1941 because of the danger of the sport, and because of the difficulty in finding equally matched opponents among rival colleges.[51]

Golf

An announcement was made by SLI in 1939 that a golf team was being organized.[52] Intercollegiate golf matches, played at the Lafayette Municipal Course,[53] increased the interest in golf among area residents.

Track

A track team was organized in 1911. The success of this sport at Southwestern was so great by the mid-twenties that Southwestern began a track carnival. The First Annual Southwestern Institute Relays Carnival, held in 1928, involved 400 athletes representing 9 colleges from Louisiana, Mississippi and Texas, and 28 Louisiana high schools.[54] Anyone who is familiar with athletics at Southwestern is familiar with the Southwestern Relays held each spring.

Gymnastics

A gymnastic team was organized in 1940 as a part of the athletic program.[55] This sport offered students unable to qualify for other sports an opportunity to participate in intercollegiate athletic competition.

During 1939 Southwestern instituted the Southwestern Hall of Fame. President Frazar began the organizational move.[56] The purpose of the Hall of Fame is to

honor these men, past present, and future, who, by their deeds as players and leaders, and by their example of their lives, personify the great contributions of athletics to our way of life. Their names shall be enshrined forever in the Hall of Fame.

Membership required the following:

1. Athletic achievement must be solely the result of intercollegiate participation. This intercollegiate achievement must be characterized by outstanding performances and recognition for approximately two years.
2. Scholarship and campus leadership must be of the highest order.
3. To be eligible, athletes must have been graduated at least five years.
4. A history of the athlete's accomplishments must be submitted to the Faculty Athletic Committee. Upon the Committee's recommendation and the approval of the President of Southwestern Louisiana Institute, the athlete's name and photograph shall be placed in the Hall of Fame.
5. Only one name shall be approved in a year.[57]

The USL Athletic Hall of Fame consists of

Gustave Trahan (1924)
Edward J. Richardson (1925)
Alton Moss Bujard (1926)
Christian "Red" Cagle (1926)
R. J. "Tom" Cambre (1926)
Clifton J.Theriot (1926)
E. Glynn Abel (1930)
John W. Morriss (1930)
P. W. "Bordy" Bordelon (1931)
J. Otto Broussard (1931)
Dudly G. Wilkins (1936)
Louie A. Campbell (1938)
Joe E. Johnson (1939)
Carrol R. Baggett (1931)
Carl R. Hurst (1941)
Donald H. Fisher (1950)
George William Crowson (1951)[58]

The 1940-41 school session is outstanding in Southwestern's athletic history. Southwestern's football team coached by John Cain, placed first in the Louisiana Intercollegiate Conference; the basketball team, coached by J. C. Reinhardt, tied for first with Louisiana Normal; the track team, coached by Robert Browne, placed first; the tennis team coached by Professor McDavid of the English department tied for first; Coach Cliff Johnson's baseball team finished second; and Professor Mallison's golf team finished second.[59]

During World War II Southwestern's athletic activities were reduced because of the great number of students in the armed forces: The football team lost 7 of its leading players, the basketball team lost 6 of its 9-man team, and the track team lost all of its sprinters.[60] In the later years of World War II, the 6 Louisiana colleges of the LIC excluded all athletic activities for the 1942-43 session to "devote all their energies to well-balanced physical education courses."[61] Following the war years Southwestern's athletic program was reactivated.

Organization of an Intramural Sports Program for men at Southwestern in 1950 provided

an opportunity for organized play in all sports, both team and individual, to all students who are not members of varsity or B team squads in that activity.[62]

The major sports included touch football, boxing, basketball, track and field, softball, and volleyball. The Athletic Department supervised the intramural sports activities for fraternity and independent groups, its objective being "A SPORT FOR EVERY MAN AND EVERY MAN IN A SPORT."[63]

The athletic activity at Southwestern developed steadily until 1960, with the 1940-41 year as a high mark. Since then continued organization of the athletic program has been made. The growth and development of Southwestern's athletic activities during its first sixty-year history – along with conversion from industrial institute (1900-1921), to a liberal arts college (1921) to a university (1960) – cannot be overlooked as it provided both Southwestern and Lafayette with wholesome athletic competition. Just as Southwestern sought to provide academic excellence, so did she attempt to provide an organized athletic program enjoyed by students, faculty, alumni, and residents of Acadiana. The main ingredient in Southwestern's athletic program is gradual improvement which has enabled Southwestern to become a feared opponent among its athletic rivals.

CHAPTER VII

STUDENT LIFE

Southwestern's students almost always seem to have had a good time. Sometimes this enjoyment ran counter to the purposes and intentions of the administration, and invariably, whenever students and administration clashed, students came out second best. Nevertheless, students apparently enjoyed their lives at Southwestern and their association with the faculty and administration has been unusually close.

The close relationship between student and administration at Southwestern is a result of sage planning of rules and regulations which have governed the lives of the students. The demerit system was used to discipline the young men until 1910. This strict military disciplinary system at Southwestern during the formative period is illustrated in the following regulations:

Disobedience	Demerits
Spilling sugar on the cafeteria floor	2
Visiting in dormitory during study hours	2
Spilling gravy at the cafeteria table	2
Improper dress in dormitory halls	2
Unmade bed in dormitory	2[1]

Strict discipline was the rule at the Industrial Institute. The strict wording of a letter from a concerned parent to President Stephens stating, "Put the Rod to him if he needs it, I sent him to you to make a man out of him,"[2] clearly illustrates the role of strict discipline at Southwestern during its early years.

The young ladies' activities were also carefully supervised. Girls were not to stay off campus overnight, and were especially to refrain from walking on the sidewalks of Lafayette with boys. President Stephens wrote to the parent of a girl who had disobeyed this rule:

If they walk with young men on the streets of Lafayette (which is positively forbidden) we place the entire blame upon them. They could, of course, avoid it.[3]

Young coeds at Southwestern enjoying themselves despite their heavy clothing.

Southwestern Archives

An interesting observation about the supervision of girls at Southwestern as told by A. Wilmot Dalferes, student at the Industrial Institute, 1913-1916, is that "Girls were treated like prisoners!" A particular observation he recollected was the supervision of the girls attending the literary society meetings on campus held in the evenings in Martin Hall. The girl students were individually checked by head count as they left the dormitory (DeClouet Hall), entered Martin Hall, left Martin Hall, and reentered the dormitory – four times.[4] This was close supervision.

Summer school rules for 1909 again exemplify the strict discipline which limited the young ladies' activities.

1. Young ladies are required to be at the dormitories in which they room, not later than 7:30 p.m. every day, except by special permission of the President or Matron.
2. The only time for receiving young gentlemen callers will be on Sunday afternoons and evenings, not earlier than 5 nor later than 9 o'clock. The "going" bell will ring at nine. There will be no objection to promenades, iced cream, moving pictures and such things during the weekdays, provided the 7:30 p.m. rule (No. 1) is strictly observed.
3. The only places to receive callers are the reception rooms and the galleries of the dormitories. No noise, remember, after 7:30 p.m. Lights out and front doors locked at 10 p.m. No dancing or card playing in the dormitories.[5]

The Library rules in 1909 were strict.

1. No talking in the library.
2. No reference books or current periodicals may be taken out.
3. No student is allowed to take out more than a book at a time – except by special permission of a teacher whose work requires the use of this extra book.
4. No book may be kept out more than two weeks.
5. At the end of that time the book may be renewed provided there has been no demand for it in the meantime.

6. No student is allowed to remove books from the shelves. He must apply to the Librarian.
7. The Library is open from 3:25 until 4 p.m. on all school days.[6]

Many of the rules applicable to the students of Southwestern during its early years are not applicable today. In 1906 the use of tobacco was forbidden and the students were given the choice of "quitting the weed or leaving school."[7] This rule would be almost impossible to enforce today.

Southwestern discontinued military discipline as a part of its educational program in 1910. No longer would the men students (cadets) have to undergo vigorous military drill or purchase uniforms.[8] Southwestern temporarily resumed military training, however, on the eve of World War I. Through President Stephens' efforts Southwestern became one of the Student Army Training Corps centers in 1917. In order to qualify for the SATC division, Southwestern had to recruit at least 100 draft-eligible men between the ages of 18 and 45 with a high school education as a minimum requirement. The SATC program was a result of the "desire of the War Department that whatever practicable military instructions be given at all educational institutions."[9] The SATC Division was subsequently demobilized in 1919 following World War I because its purpose had ended.[10]

During World War I the students of Southwestern responded to President Woodrow Wilson's appeal to educational institutions to aid the local draft boards. Southwestern's students were sent to the Lafayette Parish Courthouse to make vocational cards of men eligible for the draft.[11] The girls of Southwestern further aided the war effort by providing Americans in Europe with handmade knitwear. These included wash clothes, wristlets, helmets, mufflers, socks and sweaters.[12] Pecan trees were planted on campus in 1920 as a memorial to Southwestern students killed while serving their country during the war.[13]

The 1921-22 *Catalog* provided for revised regulations which were not military and not as strict as the earlier ones.

Young men boarding at Southwestern were required to remain in their dormitories from the beginning of study hour (about seven o'clock) until the breakfast hour in the morning; permission was required to leave the campus. Dormitory rooms were to be cleaned every day. On Sundays an assembly of all male boarders was held before they attended church services in groups.[14]

Young ladies were under the supervision of a carefully selected matron. They were not permitted "at any time" to spend the night away from the dormitory, and were "expected to attend services" at their respective churches on Sundays.[15]

The social activities of the students of Southwestern in 1923 were governed by the Faculty Committee on Student Organizations. This committee had

supervision of every social function given by the Institute or by any organization within, including fraternities, sororities and other student activities.[16]

The Student Association of Southwestern Louisiana Institute was organized following Southwestern's reorganization as a four-year liberal arts college in 1921. Its purpose was

to further the interest of the students of Southwestern Institute (and) to cooperate with the authorities of Southwestern Louisiana Institute in matters of general welfare.

The extracurricular organizations available to Southwestern students by 1924 were:

Religions organizations: YWCA, YMCA, Newman Club
French and Latin Clubs
Attakapas and Avatar Literary Societies
Southwestern Social Service Society-service organization
"S" Club – SLI athletic lettermen
Women's Athletic Association
Piano Club

An unidentified freshman at Southwestern. He is wearing the freshman cap typical of the days when Southwestern had Freshman Initiation.
Southwestern Archives

Glee Club
Social Sororities and Fraternities
Dramatic Club
Publications: *The Vermilion, L'Acadien, Side Lights*
(Publication for Alumni), and the *Southwestern
Handbook.*[17]

Freshman initiation, an activity which orients freshmen to college, became an important phase of Southwestern's student life activities. Freshman initiation activities in 1929 included for the first time the clipping of the hair of freshmen students "presumably by upper classmen." This was immediately forbidden by the administration as a "practice prohibited by colleges and universities in general," even though the hair cutting "did not meet with much opposition."[18] Following an investigation President Stephens announced:

Five men students of Southwestern Institute have been dismissed and a sixth is under suspended dismissal, as a result of the recent Freshmen "hair clipping" at the college....[19]

Freshman initiation subsequently lost its backing by the administration and the initiation activities diminished. Freshman regulations were revised in 1938, and included:

1. Freshman caps must be worn at all times until Thanksgiving. This includes out-of-town trips.
2. Freshmen are not allowed to walk on the grass on Campus.
3. Freshmen must attend all athletic contests and pep meetings.
4. Freshmen must obey all orders within reasonable limits, such as carrying laundry, cleaning rooms, shining shoes, etc.
5. Freshmen will not be disturbed during study hour, and they in turn will disturb no one.
6. All high school letters must be removed. No letter may be worn except the Southwestern "S".
7. Freshmen are expected to learn the Alma Mater and the Southwestern yells and songs.

8. Any student having completed his freshman year in another senior college will not be treated as a freshman, but will not have privileges of an upper classman until he has been a student at Southwestern for a session of nine months.
9. Ignorance of these rules will not be considered as an excuse for violation of them.
10. Violations of these rules will be promptly and effectively dealt with.[20]

During Lether Frazar's administration plans for the construction of a student center were announced. This building was designed as the center for student activities. It contained recreation rooms, lounges, a refectory, a post office and a bookstore needed to accommodate Southwestern's expanding needs.[21] This gave the students a meeting place and a social center.

The Students of Southwestern became as actively involved with World War II as they had with the first World War. The college again provided military training on the campus during this war. Students of SLI were eligible to join the Army Air Corps, Naval Air Corps, Naval Reserve, Marine Reserve or the Army Reserve. Training was offered to men students in math, science, English, history, and physical education. One hour of physical education per day was required.[22]

The Navy also had a training program at Southwestern during World War II. The program consisted of basic training for approximately 700 Navy men. The program was named the V-12 Program and enabled freshmen and sophomores from seventeen to nineteen to spend two calendar years at Southwestern while doing passing work. After these two years, the Navy V-1 comprehensive exam was given to determine if the student would continue college under the V-7 flight training program or become immediately an apprentice seaman. The Navy training program at Southwestern during World War II was coordinated by Dr. Hollis Long of the Southwestern faculty, and prevented Southwestern from being closed for lack of students. The program brought over 700 young men to Southwestern, an addition which greatly boosted the previous enrollment of 120 men students.[23]

An Air Force ROTC class at Southwestern. ROTC began in 1948 on the campus.

Southwestern Archives

The return of the veterans of World War II created new problems for Southwestern's administration. Difficulties existed in providing adequate dormitory space for Southwestern's 281 GI students. By the fall of 1946 there were 1,700 veterans pursuing the fifty-nine courses of study at Southwestern.[24]

Emphasis on military training has always been important at Southwestern. Plans were made for a Reserve Officer Training Corps at Southwestern as early as 1919.[25] These plans were futile. In 1939 another application was made by President Frazar for an ROTC unit at Southwestern. The second attempt for a unit was begun by the Lafayette Stanley Martin American Legion Post No. 69.[26] It was not, however, before 1948 that Southwestern was accepted as an Air Force Reserve Officer Training Corps Center.[27] Southwestern still maintains an Air Force ROTC Unit on its campus.

Student publications were another important phase of student life. These publications recorded student activities through the years. The college newspaper, *The Vermilion*, and the annual, the *L'Acadien*, best express the college life of the students at Southwestern. *The Vermilion*, first published in 1904, contained primarily school news and increased in subscription from 125 to 225 copies during the 1914-15 session.[28] This represented a large increase in subscriptions compared to its first ten years of publication. The student paper grew in scope simultaneously with Southwestern and was cited by the University of Minnesota and the National Inter-collegiate Press Association in 1939 as a first-class college newspaper.[29]

Southwestern's first *L'Acadien*, published in 1912, was dedicated to Robert Martin,[30] St. Martin legislator who introduced in the Louisiana House of Representatives the bill which subsequently established Southwestern. The annual was compiled and published mainly by the graduating class of Southwestern.[31] In 1919, the *L'Acadien* ceased publication because of the great expense of paper during the war;[32] publication was resumed in 1920.

Three of the dormitories which formed the Agriculture Student Center. The dirt road in the foreground is Woodson Street today.

Southwestern Archives

In the late 1920s, the late Edith Garland Dupré, then Head of the English Department sponsored a magazine of verse, *The Circle,* which lasted until the Depression of the thirties. In 1929, this student publication was revived by Mary Dichmann, Head of Southwestern's English Department. Called the *Scribbler's Script,* it was designed "to encourage literary endeavors among students on the campus." This publication was also short-lived, and in the winter of 1956 another student publication, *Some SLI Writers,* was begun and was essentially the same as Southwestern's present student publication, *Exile.*[33]

Another publication which is an important tool for freshmen is the *Southwestern Handbook.* The first handbook for Southwestern students was published in 1939 by the Newman club. This handbook contained

information concerning all organizations on the degree campus, football schedules, freshmen regulations, church directory and other helpful information.[34]

A program for student employment began in 1929 at Southwestern as a result of the need for financial support by some of the students. It consisted of jobs as athletic aids, positions on the *L'Acadien* and *The Vermilion,* and other services such as working in the Post Office or the library. By 1930, 103 students participated in Southwestern's Student Employment Program.[35]

Another program to provide an opportunity to men students who were in financial need began in 1936 by Professor Joel Lafayette Fletcher, then Head of the Southwestern Agriculture Department and later President of Southwestern. This program enabled a young man to attend Southwestern while making thirteen dollars a month either from the cultivation of farm products or labor. The dormitory space for the first fifty-six students in the program was provided through Work Progress Administration funds. The farm-education program was praised because

The Catholic Student Center's original buildings were completed in 1942. This was the first religious center on campus.
Southwestern Archives

the often-dreamed and often-promised goal of education, college training within the reach of everyone, is becoming a reality at Southwestern Louisiana Institute at Lafayette.[36]

By November 1937 a third dormitory was being built to accommodate the 306 students in the program[37] which included work on the agriculture farm, the dairy farm, janitorial work, aid to professors, and work on the nursery project.[38] Cooperative Boarding Club students also cultivated a large part of their food on the campus farm, thus decreasing their expenses.[39]

A placement service formed at Southwestern in 1942 introduced prospective seniors to possible employers. Personal and educational history of the student was kept on file[40] to provide ready reference and quick placement service. This service aided Southwestern's students in learning about potential employment. This service is still provided to students at Southwestern.

Religious activity has been an important part of Southwestern's history. Over half of the students enrolled at Southwestern were Catholic in the mid-thirties. In 1937, a group of Catholic leaders in Lafayette, headed by Felix H. Mouton, began a financial drive for building a Catholic Student Center. Donations were sought from throughout southwest Louisiana.[41] In 1949 Reverend C. J. Gaudin, Chaplain of the Southwestern Newman Club, stated that the fundamental purpose of the Newman Club was "to inspire and keep alive in the individual a wholesome spiritual life."[42]

Plans were announced in 1941 for building a $50,000 Center and Chapel for Catholic students on the Southwestern campus.[43] The first mass at Our Lady Seat of Wisdom Chapel was celebrated on March 1, 1942, by Reverend Paul M. Fuselier, Pastor.[44]

Baptist students at Southwestern were also organizing by 1940. They planned to attend the Baptist Student Union convention at Louisiana Polytechnic Institute in that year. The purpose was to organize recreation for the Baptist students at Southwestern.[45]

By 1941 there were five religious organizations represented on the Southwestern campus. These were the Baptist Student Union, the Craig Morris League (Episcopal), the Newman Club (Catholic), the Presbyterian Student Association, and the Wesley Foundation (Methodist).[46]

There were also several Greek organizations on campus by 1933. Local social fraternities were Alpha Sigma Kappa, Phi Kappa Alpha, Sigma Pi Alpha and Tau Sigma Delta. Local social sororities were Delta Sigma Nu, Delta Theta Sigma, Nu Sigma Kappa, and Phi Delta Epsilon. Sigma Sigma Sigma was the only national social-education sorority on campus.[47] A second national social sorority, Alpha Sigma Alpha, was organized in 1940.[48]

Southwestern's first national social fraternity was organized in 1941. Through the leadership of F. Xavier Mouton, Alumni of the LSU Chapter, the Phi Kappa Theta chapter of Theta Kappa Phi was founded at Southwestern. Theta Kappa Phi was not only the first national social fraternity, but it was also a fraternity of Catholic men.[49] By the late fifties Southwestern had four national fraternities: Delta Sigma Phi, Kappa Sigma, Theta Kappa Phi (Phi Kappa Theta), and Theta Xi; and one local fraternity, Alpha Sigma Kappa. There were three national sororities at this time: Alpha Sigma Alpha, Sigma Sigma Sigma, and Delta Delta Delta; and six local sororities: Delta Epsilon Nu (Kappa Delta), Delta Theta Sigma (Alpha Omicron Pi), Nu Sigma Kappa (Delta Zeta), Phi Delta Epsilon (Phi Mu), Delta Sigma Delta and Delta Sigma Kappa.[50]

Aside from social organizations Southwestern also had several honorary, service, and professional organizations on campus by 1940. Southwestern was notified in April, 1932, that it had been accepted by the National Blue Key fraternity as one of its colonies. Herbert A. Hamilton was instrumental in the success of Southwestern's petition to the national organization.[51] Dr. R. W. Porter, Professor of Psychology, was the Club's first advisor.[52] The Blue Key Directory which contains addresses and phone numbers of the faculty and students and is published at Southwestern today is spearheaded by Vernon Bell, Chairman of the Blue Key project in 1938.[53]

109

Nu Sigma Kappa was one of the local social sororities on campus. This local was later affiliated with Delta Zeta, National social sorority.

Southwestern Archives

Southwestern has always had commuters. As a result of the many commuter students, in 1937 a Girls' Club was provided by Southwestern to the girls from the surrounding area who motored daily to Lafayette. The club room which was the center of activity was located in Martin Hall.[54]

To provide for the specific needs of Southwestern's students, several organizations sprouted on campus. Alpha Phi Omega, Southwestern's first national service fraternity for men was organized in 1939.[55] International appeal on the campus in 1939-40 was reflected in Puerto Rican and Latin clubs formed at Southwestern.[56] Service organizations and international clubs were supplemented with honor societies. Phi Gamma Mu, national honor society for social science students with high scholastic standing, was organized in 1927 with an initial membership of 22.[57] The Delta Iota Chapter of Kappa Delta Pi, national education honor society, was formed in 1935.[58] In 1941, Pi Delta Phi, national honorary French fraternity, was installed; and in 1954 Phi Alpha Theta, national honor society in history was organized.[59]

Some of the professional fraternities on the campus by 1950 were Alpha Chi (chemistry), Demeter Club (agriculture), Sigma Alpha Gamma (agriculture majors fraternity), Pi Kappa Delta (debating and oratory fraternity),[60] and the Louisiana Engineering Society.[61]

The Dean of Men, Rex McCullogh, and S. A. McNeely of the Physical Education Department made a survey in 1940 to determine the characteristics of the average Southwestern man. The average Southwestern man of 1940 was described as being five feet nine inches tall, on the slender side weighing one hundred forty-four pounds, with white and shiny teeth. As a rule the average Southwestern man did not wear glasses, had a good sense of hearing, a sound heart, was eighteen years and seven months old, and disapproved of girls who smoked or drank.[62] The average Southwestern man is always changing.

By the late fifties the students of Southwestern were more socially oriented than the students of earlier years and were

111

able to join several organizations on campus to complement their educational training.[63] Participating in extracurricular activities introduced the student to social etiquette among other young adults, and also provided for the acquaintance of new friends. Social, professional, service, honorary, and military organizations became the hub of student life because of the friendships which developed as a result of studying and socializing. The larger the enrollment, the greater the need for organizations to provide the students with activities in addition to academic studies.

Organizations sprouted rapidly on Southwestern's campus. Through the guidance of the Faculty Committee on Student Organizations, the activities of the numerous student organizations were planned to produce the most good for the students. As a result of the sage organization of student activities by the faculty and administration, Southwestern's students almost always had a good time.

Southwestern's students could join numerous campus
organizations by the late fifties.

Honorary and Professional Organizations

Phi Kappa Delta – Debating
Phi Gamma Mu – Social Science
Lambda Omega – Women freshmen scholarship
Arnold Air Society
Pi Lambda Beta – Pre-Law
Kappa Delta Pi – Education
Phi Kappa Phi – General Honor
Sigma Gamma Epsilon – Geology
Sigma Alpha Beta – Speech Correction
Sigma Alpha Iota – Women's Music
Sigma Theta – Home Economics
Sigma Delta Pi – Spanish
Kappa Mu Epsilon – Mathematics
Phi Mu Alpha Sinfonia – Men's Music
Vermilion Honor Society
Alpha Psi Omega – Dramatics
Phi Alpha Theta – Social Studies
Sigma Tau Delta – English
Pi Delta Phi – French

Departmental and Technical Organizations

Le Cercle Français
"S" Club
Physical Education Majors Club
Women's Recreational Association
Demeter (Agriculture)
SAH (Agriculture)
American Chemical Society
Orchesis – Dance
Future Teachers of America
Geological Society
Accounting Forum
Louisiana Engineering Society
Art Club
Southwest Society of Civil Engineers
Southwest Society of Petroleum Engineers

113

Southwest Architectural Society

Religious Organizations

Cantebury Club (Episcopal)
Wesley Foundation (Methodist)
Newman Club (Roman Catholic)
Westminster Fellowship (Presbyterian)
Interfaith Council
Baptist Student Union

Leadership and Service Organizations

Alpha Phi Omega – National Service Fraternity for men
Blue Key – National Leadership fraternity
Circle K
Red Jackets
SOHS – organization for Higher Standards

Activities

Publications
Varsity and Intramurals
Cultural-Music-Theatrical
Football
Basketball
Baseball
Tennis
Golf
Track

Handbook, 1956-57, pp. 30-33; *L'Acadien*, 1956, pp. 176-191; and
Bradley Quoyser, ed. *Introducing Fraternities at S. L. I.,*
Lafayette, SLI, 1956, pp. 15-20.

Dupre Library (rear view) was named in honor of a Southwest Louisiana family of which Edith Garland Dupre, a member of the original faculty and longtime English professor at Southwestern, was a member.

Southwestern Archives

CHAPTER VIII

EPILOGUE 1960-1966

In 1961 the University of Southwestern Louisiana was invited to join the Southern University Conference. This Association is composed of 56 colleges and universities in 14 states.[1] Its members include institutions of higher learning that have attained high academic standards. Tulane, Louisiana State University and Southwestern are the only Louisiana institutions of higher learning that have become members. Former President Fletcher speaks of Southwestern's membership in the Conference as "the most important development in the 25 years I spent there as president."[2]

Considerable physical expansion has also occurred since 1960. This has included the construction of over 90,000 sq. feet of floor space over the existing Dupré Library facility, a new administration building (Martin Hall), the construction of a new mathematics and education building, (Maxim D. Doucet Hall); a three-million dollar medical arts facility, (Vernon L. Wharton hall); a music building, (Angelle Hall); a new dining hall, (Esteve Martin Hall); a commerce building, (Franklin G. Mouton Hall); and several women dormitories, (Rexford C. McCullough Dorm, Edward G. Voorhies Dorm, William B. Stokes Dorm, Anna Marshall Denbo Dorm, and Anne Delie Bancroft Dorm). A new student union facility is presently under construction. These are representative of Southwestern's growth during the sixties.

In 1964, a move was begun by the Fletcher administration to acquire the New Iberia Naval Auxiliary Air Station which would have increased Southwestern's total campus with the addition of a 4,300 acre site with a total of $19 million in buildings.[3]

In June, 1965, the Naval Auxiliary Air Station was officially turned over to the University of Southwestern Louisiana, and Clyde L. Rougeau, Dean of Animal Husbandry, was named to head the New Iberia branch (which was to be a freshman division of the University). At this ceremony Fletcher praised this move as

116

New Martin Hall, named in honor of Robert Martin-the Louisiana legislator who introduced the bill which established Southwestern, is Southwestern's administration building.

Southwestern Archives

Southwestern's mathematics and education building was named for Maxim D. Doucet, former Dean of Education.
Southwestern Archives

Southwestern's music building, Angelle Hall, was named in honor of a southwest Louisiana Family. Ex-legislator Robert "Bob" Angelle was influential in providing the necessary funds for the construction.

Southwestern Archives

Anna Marshall Denbo Hall and Anne Delie Bancroft Hall are two of Southwestern's women's dormitories. These dormitories were named in honor of two women influential in Southwestern's history.　　Southwestern Archives

a memorable occasion, for today Southwestern really becomes a regional university, prepared to serve more effectively all of the children of this rich and populous area for which it was created.[4]

The proposal for a branch of the University in New Iberia caused considerable controversy. Opponents to the move of freshmen students to New Iberia emphasized the "detriment to the cause of education as well as to the economy of Lafayette," in areas of accreditation, funds, economics, library facilities, commuter distances, and the problems of a split-administration.[5]

In addition to the criticism of Lafayette citizens, Fletcher and W. E. Whetstone, President of the State Board of Education, disagreed as to the exact purpose of the New Iberia branch. Fletcher insisted that the State Board of Education had given USL permission to transfer all freshmen students to New Iberia; while Whetstone stated that Southwestern could use the New Iberia base for educational purposes, but no permission had been given USL to open a lower division of only freshmen at New Iberia.[6]

Fletcher's determination to attain the New Iberia branch to improve Southwestern's academic and physical plant was criticized by Louisiana businessmen. In September, 1965, the Lafayette Chamber of Commerce charged the Fletcher administration with

trying to depict the citizens of Lafayette as evil, selfish and mercenary people, and they are making an attempt to turn the neighboring parishes against the people of Lafayette.[7]

In defense of Fletcher's administration the late Muriel McCulla Price of Southwestern's English department wrote the following to the *Daily Advertiser*:

When a man like President Joel L. Fletcher who has demonstrated many times over and for many years his vision, integrity, vitality and faithful leadership in this area

121

Clyde L Rougeau became Southwestern's fourth president in 1966.
Southwestern Archives

can be persecuted by an ungrateful public, I say that the great Christian virtue of gratitude is much diminished among us.[8]

The resignation of President Joel L. Fletcher in October, 1965, was a surprise to some of the members of the State Board of Education. Dr. Joseph Riehl, vice-president for academic affairs, resigned simultaneously. Fletcher said he resigned in order to allay criticism for the plan for expansion into New Iberia. The fact that he was past retirement age and the mounting public criticism of his administration engendered by the New Iberia controversy contributed to his decision for retirement. In addition, his retirement at this time enabled him to participate in the selection of his successor.[9] Clyde L. Rougeau was appointed by the Board to replace Fletcher as Southwestern's president. At the time, Fletcher said Rougeau's appointment "meets with my great approval." Rougeau, Dean of Animal Husbandry, and appointed head of the proposed New Iberia branch, served as acting president of Southwestern from January to July 1966. A native of Lecompte, Louisiana, he received his bachelor's degree in agriculture from SLI, his master's degree from Texas A &M, and his doctorate degree from the University of Minnesota.[10] As Southwestern's fourth president, Rougeau was challenged by the administration of a growing and restless university.

The Lafayette *Daily Advertiser* described the Board's action on the okaying of the New Iberia branch as:

It was only a half dozen of the 11-man board that railroaded through a piece of curious action filled with holes and devoid of responsibility.[11]

Steps for making the New Iberia branch an Education Center were continued despite criticism. Recommendations to the Board of Education requested the freshmen year towards a bachelor's degree and one and two-year technical curricula which would entitle the student completing this study an associate in arts or associate in science degrees.[12]

In December, 1965 Lafayette parish residents represented by Robert L. Kleinpeter of Baton Rouge and the law office of Domengeaux and Wright of Lafayette filed suit against the State Board of Education stating that:

The board's action is illegal and unconstitutional...in seeking an injunction against the board to set up a branch of the university 13 miles from Lafayette....

The establishment of a branch was argued as being unconstitutional because of the Louisiana Constitution's prohibition that

no new educational institution can be established by the state except upon two-thirds vote of the Legislature.[13]

Two months later a court ruling from the 19th District Court in Baton Rouge issued by Judge Fred Blanche

permanently enjoined the State Board of Education and USL from establishing such a facility at the site of the old Naval Air Auxiliary Station near New Iberia.[14]

It was decided that this move would bring "chaos and bankruptcy to the educational system of Louisiana" by permitting institutions of higher learning to establish branches in any parish they might decide.[15] The decision was then appealed to the Louisiana Supreme Court.

In February, 1967, the Supreme Court of Louisiana upheld the District Court's decision and stated that the

establishment of the branch by resolution and without legislative authorization violated the state constitution.[16]

Thus ended Southwestern's proposed New Iberia branch. In the turmoil, Southwestern had acquired a new president, Clyde Rougeau, who now turned his efforts toward developing the Lafayette campus in building for the future.

The New Iberia branch may have benefitted Southwestern by increasing its campus facilities tremendously. A split-administration, however, might have harmed Southwestern's academic growth in that USLNI might have been undesirable to freshmen students; thus causing a decrease in enrollment. No one can say what might have been, yet true to the early days of Southwestern, Lafayette once again proved capable of maintaining priority over New Iberia in making Lafayette the home of the University of Southwestern Louisiana.

BIBLIOGRAPHY

Documents

Acts Passed by the General Assembly of the State of Louisiana at the Regular Session Begun and Held in the City of Baton Rouge on the Sixteenth Day of May 1898. Baton Rouge: The Advocate, 1898.

Constitution and ByLaws of the Southwestern Louisiana Industrial Institute Alumni Association, Lafayette Louisiana. Lafayette: Lafayette Advertiser, 1905.

Constitution of the State of Louisiana, Adopted May 12, 1892; With Amendments Including the Extra Session of the Louisiana Legislature held August 12, 1912. Annotated by Theodore Contonio. New Orleans: Louisiana Publishing Co., 1913.

Louisiana Legislature. *Acts Passed by the Legislature of the State of Louisiana at the Regular Session Begun and Held in the City of Baton Rouge on the Eleventh Day of May, 1936.* Published by the Authority of the State of Louisiana, 1936.

Louisiana Legislature. *Acts Passed by the Legislature of the State of Louisiana at the Regular Session Begun and Held in the City of Baton Rouge on the Thirteenth Day of May, 1940.* Published by the Authority of the State of Louisiana, 1940.

Official Journal of the Proceedings of the House of Representatives of the State of Louisiana at the First Regular Session of the Fifth General Assembly, Begun and Held in the City of Baton Rouge, May 11, 1896. Baton Rouge: Advocate, 1896.

Official Journal of the Proceedings of the Senate of the State of Louisiana at the Second Regular Session Begun and Held in the City of Baton Rouge, May 16, 1898. Baton Rouge: Advocate, 1898.

BIBLIOGRAPHY

BOOKS

Carter, Hodding. *Louisiana Almanac, 1968.* New Orleans: Pelican Publishing House. 1968.

Cline, Rodney. *Builders of Louisiana Education.* Baton Rouge: Bureau of Educational Materials and Research, College of Education, Louisiana, 1963.

Cook, Robert C. and Eleanor Carrol. (eds.) *Trustees and Presidents of American Colleges and Universities, 1955-56.* Nashville: Who's Who in American Education, Inc., 1955.

Davis, Edwin Adams. *The Story of Louisiana.* Vol. I. New Orleans: J. F. Hyer Publishing Co., 1960.

Fay, Edwin Whitfield. *The History of Education in Louisiana.* Washington: Government Printing Office, 1898.

Fortier, Alcee. (ed.) *Louisiana; Comprising Sketches of Parishes, Towns, Events, Institutions, and Persons, Arranged in Cyclopedic Form.* Vol. I. Madison, Wisconsin: Century Historical Association, 1914.

Harris, Thomas H. *The Story of Public Education in Louisiana.* New Orelans: Delgado Trades School, 1924.

Robertson, Minns Sledge. *Public Education in Louisiana After 1898.* Baton Rouge: Louisiana State University Press, 1952.

Sindler, Allan P. *Huey Long's Louisiana: State Politics, 1920-1952.* Baltimore, Johns Hopkins Press, 1956.

Wilkerson, Marcus M. *Thomas Duckett Boyd; the Story of a Southern Educator.* Baton Rouge: Louisiana State University Press, 1935.

Williamson, Frederick. *Origin and Growth of Agricultural Extension in Louisiana—1860-1948; How it Opened the*

Road for Progress in Better Farming and Rural Living. Baton Rouge: Louisiana State University, Division of Agricultural Extension, 1951.

Article and Periodicals

Beaumont Enterprise, 1939-1940.

Crowley Signal, 1904-1905.

Daily Advertiser, 1900-1967.

Daily Iberian, 1946.

Daily States [New Orleans], 1900-1958.

Fletcher, Joel Lafayette. "The First President, Edwin Lewis Stephens and the Early Years of Southwestern Louisiana Institute." Lafayette: University of Southwestern Louisiana, September.

Jochem, Margaret Stephens. "The Life Story of Edwin Lewis Stephens," *The Southwestern Louisiana Journal,* IV, January, 1960.

L'Acadien, 1914.

Lafayette Gazette, 1900-1921.

Lafayette Progress, 1939-1940, 1948, 1957.

Monroe News Star, 1938.

Starr, Harris E. (ed.) *Dictionary of American Biography.* 22 Vols. New York: Charles Scribner's Sons, 1964.

Southwestern Louisiana Institute, "Faculty Biographical Sketches," 1940.

BIBLIOGRAPHY

Southwestern Louisiana Institute Handbook, 1956-57. Lafayette, Louisiana, 1956, University of Southwestern Louisiana.

Southwestern Louisiana Institute: A Self Study, 1958-59. Lafayette, Louisiana, 1959, University of Southwestern Louisiana.

University of Southwestern Louisiana Biennial Reports, 1902-1960. Lafayette, Louisiana, University of Southwestern Louisiana.

University of Southwestern Louisiana Catalog, 1900-1960. Lafayette, Louisiana, University of Southwestern Louisiana.

University of Southwestern Louisiana Institute Bulletin, 1900-1960. Lafayette, Louisiana, University of Southwestern Louisiana.

Stephens, Edwin Lewis. "Education in Louisiana in the Closing Decades of the Nineteenth Century," *Louisiana Historical Quarterly*, XVI (January, 1933).

Stephens, Edwin Lewis. "The Story of Acadian Education in Louisiana." *Louisiana Historical Quarterly*, XVIII (April, 1935).

Times Picayune [New Orleans] , 1900-1960.

Vermilion, 1904-1966.

Unpublished Theses and Dissertations

Childress, Ora (Michael). "Edwin Lewis Stephens; Scholar and Educator." Typewritten Copy to Stephens Memorial Library by President Joel L. Stephens, 1948.

Faulk, John W. "The History of Education in Lafayette Parish, Louisiana." Unpublished Master's dissertation, Department of Elementary Education, Louisiana State University, 1933.

Jochem, Margaret Stephens. "A History of Southwestern Louisiana Institute; 1900-1936." Unpublished Master's dissertation, Department of English, George Peabody College for Teachers, 1937.

Kennedy, Florence. "Edwin Lewis Stephens' Influence on Education." Research paper, 1953.

Knighten, Loma. "A History of the Library of Southwestern Louisiana Institute 1900-1948." Unpublished Master's thesis, Columbia University Graduate School, 1949.

Seale, Lea L. "Southwestern Louisiana Institute; History of the Institute Prepared for the Self-Evaluation Report for the Southern Association of Colleges and Secondary Schools." Unpublished report, University of Southwestern Louisiana, 1959-1960.

Manuscripts

Edwin Lewis Stephens, 1872-1939. Film 232. University of Southwestern Louisiana, Lafayette, Louisiana.

Joel Lafayette Fletcher Papers, Southwestern Archives and Manuscripts Collection, University of Southwestern Louisiana, Lafayette, Louisiana.

University of Southwestern Louisiana Papers, 1898-1960. 150,000 items, including inactive files and records of presidents and some departments. Total estimated volume is 450 feet. (Processing is complete to 1922). Official Records of the University. President Papers, 1900-1960. Student Life, 1901-1960. U.S.L. Scrapbooks, 1899-1960. Southwestern Archives and Manuscripts Collection, Lafayette, Louisiana.

BIBLIOGRAPHY

Interviews

Interview with Kenneth B. Hait, May 23, 1968, Lafayette, Louisiana.

Interview with James S. Bonnet, May 24, 1968, Lafayette, Louisiana.

Interview with Robert Angelle, May 25, 1968, Cecilia, Louisiana.

Interview with Joel L. Fletcher, June 14, 1968, Lafayette, Louisiana.

Interview with Miss Pearl Segura, June 14, 1968, Lafayette, Louisiana.

Interview with Joseph Riehl, June 19, 1968, Lafayette, Louisiana.

Telephone Interview with Mrs. Ruth Mouton Hamilton, July 3, 1968, Lafayette, Louisiana.

Telephone Interview with Eloi Girard, July 3, 1968, Lafayette, Louisiana.

Telephone Interview with Pothier J. Voorhies, July 3, 1968, Lafayette, Louisiana.

Telephone Interview with A. Wilmot Dalferes, July 5, 1968, Lafayette, Louisiana.

Telephone Interview with Mrs. Nathan Abramson, July 5, 1968, Lafayette, Louisiana.

Interview with Alexander G. Urban, July 9, 1968, Lafayette, Louisiana.

Interview with A. Wilmot Dalferes, July 9, 1968, Lafayette, Louisiana.

Interview with E. Glynn Abel, July 15, 1968, Lafayette, Louisiana.

Interview with Drayton Lewis, July 15, 1969, Lafayette, Louisiana.

Interview with Thomas J. Arceneaux, July 16, 1968, Lafayette, Louisiana.

Telephone Interview with Joseph Riehl, August 20, 1968, Lafayette, Louisiana.

Telephone Interview with James S. Bonnet, August 20, 1968, Lafayette, Louisiana.

Interview with Joel L. Fletcher, March 20, 1969, Lafayette, Louisiana.

APPENDIX

The Act to Create the Southwestern Louisiana Industrial Institute reads as follows:

To create and establish a State Industrial Institute for the Education of white children of the State of Louisiana in the arts and sciences.

Section 1. Be it enacted by the General Assembly of the State of Louisiana, That, a State Industrial Institute is hereby established for the education of the white children of the State of Louisiana, in the arts and sciences.

Said Institute shall be known as the 'Southwestern Louisiana Industrial Institute,' and shall be located in that parish of the 13th Senatorial District which will offer the best inducements therefor to the Board of Trustees, said location to be made by the Board to be appointed under this act, provided that the parish selected for the location of said Institution shall donate not less than twenty-five acres of land and Five Thousand Dollars to said Institution, and the same shall be organized as hereinafter provided; provided further that in case two or more of said parishes offer the same inducements then the Board of Trustees shall select, by a majority vote, the most suitable location and make report thereof to the General Assembly of the State of Louisiana, at its next session, together with such recommendations as may be conducive to the best interests of said institution.

Sec. 2. Be it further enacted, etc. That the Governor of the State shall nominate and appoint, by and with the advice and consent of the Senate, one person from each Congressional District of this State, and two from the State at large, to be trustees, and to serve as herein provided. Immediately after they shall be assembled, in consequence of their first appointment, they shall be divided by lot into two equal classes, so that the term of three of those appointed from the Congressional Districts, and one appointed from the State at large shall expire in two years, and the term of the other half shall expire in four years from the date of their appointment; so that one-half may be chosen every two years. Vacancies shall be filled as in case of other officers in

133

this State. The Governor of the State and State Superintendent of Public Education shall be ex-officio members of said Board of Trustees, and the Governor shall, when present, act as president of the Board, but the Board shall elect one of their number Vice-President. Five of the Trustees shall constitute a quorum for the transaction of business.

Sec. 3. Be it further enacted, etc., That the Board of Trustees of said Institute be and the same are hereby declared a body politic and corporate; shall be domiciled at the parish seat of the parish where the Institution will be located; shall sue and be sued, contract and be contracted with; may hold, purchase, sell and convey property, whether movable or immovable, which may be necessary or beneficial in carrying out the purposes of this act. Said Board of Trustees may provide under proper regulations and rules for conferring degrees and awarding diplomas and granting certificates, as rewards and honors for learning and skill, to the pupils of said Institute.

Sec. 4. Be it further enacted, etc., That said Board of Trustees shall fix the time or times for regular meetings, and may be convened at any time the Governor as ex-officio President may deem it expedient to do so, in order to transact business connected with said Institute.

The President of the Faculty and teachers shall be Secretary of the Board of Trustees, and he shall keep in a well-bound book, a record of the proceedings had by said Board, and his compensation for this service shall be fixed by the Board; provided that said Board may elect a suitable person as Secretary pro tem, to act until the Institute be put in operation.

Sec. 5. Be it further enacted, etc., That the said Board of Trustees shall possess all the power necessary and proper for the accomplishment of the trust reposed in them, viz.: The establishment of a first-class Industrial Institute for the education of the white children of Louisiana in the arts and sciences, at which such children may acquire a thorough academic and literary education, together with a knowledge of kindergarten instructions, of telegraphy, stenography and photography, of drawing, painting, designing and engraving in their industrial applications; also a knowledge of fancy, practical and general needle-work; also a knowledge of bookkeeping and agricultural and mechanical art together with such other practical industries as, from time to time, may be suggested to them by experience, or such as will tend to promote the general object of said institute, to-wit: Fitting and preparing such children, male and female, for practical industries of life.

Sec. 6. Be it further enacted, etc., That the Board of Trustees shall select and appoint a president and the professors of said institute, and such other officers as they may deem necessary to put and maintain the same in successful operation, and shall make such rules and regulations for the government of said officers as they may deem advisable; they shall prescribe such a course of discipline as may be necessary to enforce the faithful discharge of the duties of all officers, professors and students. They shall prescribe the course or courses of instruction so as to secure through education and the best possible instruction in all of said industrial studies, and they shall adopt all such by-laws and regulations as they may deem necessary to carry out all the purposes and objects of said Institution.

Sec. 7. Be it further enacted, etc., That all the property acquiring in any way by said Board of Trustees shall really be the property of and belong to the State of Louisiana, but shall be held, controlled and managed by said Board of Trustees for the benefit of said Industrial Institute.

Sec. 8. Be it further enacted, etc., That said Board of Trustees shall be convened as soon as practicable.[1]

[1]*Acts Passed by the General Assembly of the State of Louisiana at the Regular Session Begun and Held in the City of Baton Rouge on the Sixteenth Day of May 1898,* (Baton Rouge: Advocate, 1898), pp. 317-319.

Private Donors

Dr. P. M. Girard....... $250	J. J. Davidson 15
Charles D. Caffery 250	C. S. Babin 25
N. P. Moss....................250	Plonsky Bros 25
S. R. Parkerson.............250	Lafayette Clothing House25
Judge Julien Mouton ...200	Pellerin Brothers 25
O. C. Mouton 200	Crescent News
I.A. Broussard 200	Hotel Co 25
A. E. Mouton................200	J. H. Knost....................25
Judge C. Debaillon 150	A. T. Caillouet...............25
William Campbell........100	Dr. H. C. Salles 25
Mouton Bros 100	Gus Schmulen 25
Mrs. P. D. Beraud 100	George Doucet 25
Dr. F. E. Girard 100	Paul Krauss 25
E. G. Voorhies.............100	George A. DeBlanc........25
D. V. Gardebled 100	Louis Lacoste 25
Dr. F. R. Tolson 100	Leon Plonsky 25
B. N. Coronna 100	Dr. J. F. Mouton............25
Rev. E. Forge 100	Mrs. P. Gerac 25
F. Demanade 100	Paul Castel 20
T. M. Boissat...............100	B. J. Pellerin..................20
J. G. Parkerson 100	L. Levy..........................20
People's	Charles Oreste Babin
Cotton Oil Co............100	(minor) 10
B. Falk............................75	J. A. Landry...................10
A. J. Ross 75	L. F. Rigues...................10
P. B. Roy........................50	Dr. J. Veazy...................10
William Clegg................50	A. B. Denbo 10
Mrs. J. S. Whittington....50	B. A. Salles 10
Dr. T. B. Hopkins...........50	J. S. Givens 5
Jules J. Mouton 50	Alex Delahoussaye...........5
Levy Bros.......................50	L. J. Serrett.....................5
Moss & Co 50	H. H. Hohorst..................5
F. K. Hopkins.................25	City Council of
F. V. Mouton.................25	Lafayette ....100[II]

[II]Scrapbook, U.S.L. Papers, S.A.M.C.

The Growth of Southwestern's Campus

Date of Acquisition	Seller	Acres	Price
3-8-1900	Crow Girard	25 acres	Gift
1-5-07	Crow Girard	25 acres	10,000
2-6-20	Mrs. Nichols, R. O. Young F. G. Mouton	109.1 acres	11,800
2-25-31	Heymann, Bendel, Caffery Mouton, Donlon	32.43 acres	10,000
8-28-36	Mary Whittington Gueriniere	171 acres	20,000
5-24-37	Lela S., M. Eloi & Clara B. Girard	12.37 acres	12,370
5-24-37	Crow Girard	13.67 acres	13,670
5-24-37	Percy M. & P. Merritt Girard	4.12 acres	4,120
6-17-37	M. Heymann	6.21 acres	5,253.03
3-8-40	Mike Donlon, Agt.	.17 acre	2,200
7-2-43	Frank G. Mouton	134.62 acres	24,312.50
10-1-44	Crow Girard	12.82 acres	46,500
10-3-44	James J. Raggio	7.18 acres	10,500
11-1-44	J. J. Foumet	21.37 acres	7,500
11-1-44	J. A. French	21.37 acres	5,500
11-1-44	Marguerite Landry Marcel Landry Marcelite Landry Laurence Landry	74.53 acres	17,440

131.79 acres Main Campus exclusive of   101,913.03
Nursery School
109.1 acres Dairy Farm   11,800.00
171 acres Whittington Farm   11,617.00
134.62 acres Mouton Farm   24,946.70
71.8 acres Raggio Farm   10,500.00
117.27 acres Others   32,952.00
735.58 $193,728.73[III]

[III]Joel L. Fletcher Papers, U.S.L. Papers, S.A.M.C.

The positions of Southwestern's faculty prior to appointment to SLII:

Victor L. Roy, Principal of Marksville High School

Ashby Woodson, Assistant Engineer at Miller Manual Training School, Albermarle Country, Virginia

Miss Gertrude Mayfield, Instructor of Domestic Science at Louisiana Industrial Institute, Ruston

Miss Beverly Randolph, Graduate of Newcomb's Art School, New Orleans

Miss Edith G. Dupré, Graduate of Newcomb and previously taught at Fairmount School, Monteagle, Tennessee

Florent Sontag, engaged as a musician at Athletic Park in New Orleans

L. W. Mayer, teacher of music at St. Landry High School

Miss Elizabeth Fowles Baker, member of prominent New Orleans family who ran a boarding house in New Orleans[IV]

[IV]The Lafayette *Gazette*, "The Industrial Institute," August 3, 1901.

One of the requirements of the Association of Southern Colleges when admitting Southwestern was the creation of a school shield. This shield, prepared by Professor Ellsworth Woodward, director of the Newcomb College Art School and Professor John M. McBryde of Tulane, is described as follows:

Quarterly, first and fourth, secure three fleur de lys argents, for France: second and third, gules a castle with three turrets machicolated and open to the field, for Spain: in chief. [sic] argent a pelican in her piety, for Louisiana

These figures stood within a circle of oak leaves characteristic of Southwest Louisiana. The Southwestern motto of "Fortiter, Feliciter, Fideliter" exemplified the educational preparation of Southwestern's students to go out into the world with courage, loyalty and gladness. The pelican on the shield is depicting a female pelican tearing its breast to revive her dead young with her own life blood.[V]

[V]Clipping, "New Shield," n.n., May 11, 1926, in U.S.L. Papers, Scrapbook, 1926-27, p. 67.

Major Construction Up to 1938

Martin Hall	$ 41,939
Foster Hall	19,589
President's Mansion	3,999
Declouet Hall	29,500
Brown Ayres Hall	13, 593
Girard Hall	40,000
Lee Hall	40,000
Buchanan and Judice Halls	121,250
Addition to Martin Hall	110,000
Oscar Kelly Allen Dining Hall	50,000
First Cooperative Dormitory	10,000
Second Cooperative Dormitory	10,000
	$469,870

Southwestern Archives and Manuscript Collection

APPENDIX

BIOGRAPHICAL SKETCH

Florent Hardy, Jr., Ph.D. has been a staff member of the Louisiana State Archives, a division of the Office of Secretary of State, since 2000 and has served as State Archivist and Director of Archival Services for years. The son of Florent Hardy, Sr. and Agnes Angelle Hardy, Dr. Hardy is a French-speaking native of the rural southwest Louisiana community of Cecilia in northern St. Martin Parish. He graduated from Cecilia High School, received a Bachelor of Arts in History, a Master of Arts in History and a Bachelor of Arts in Social Studies Education from the University of Southwestern Louisiana (University of Louisiana at Lafayette). At USL, Hardy was a member of several campus organizations and was selected to Pi Delta Phi, Honorary French Fraternity. He earned the Doctor of Philosophy in Secondary Education with a minor in History from Louisiana State University with a 4.0 GPA.

Hardy taught at Breaux Bridge Elementary, Junior High and High School as well as at the university level, and is a former employee of the State Department of Education (DOE) and the Louisiana Community and Technical College System. While at DOE, Hardy was awarded the coveted Outstanding Service Award from the Louisiana Vocational Association and the American Vocational Association. He created and edited the State Department's vocational education newsletter, *The VOICE*, a national award winner. Also while at the DOE, Hardy was a guest of the French Departments of External Affairs and Education to study the French Education System.

Hardy served as a charter member of the St. Martin Parish Chapter of the Council for the Development of French in Louisiana (CODOFIL) and is a former board member. He has served as a board member of LSU's College of Education Peabody Society and the Friends of Louisiana Public Broadcasting. He currently serves as a Board member of the Sons of the American Revolution/General Philemon Thomas Chapter, The Baton Rouge Excalibur Club, and the Louisiana Music Hall of Fame. He is a member of LSU's Friends of French Studies. He is a founding member of his Great Uncle's Auguste "Nonco" Pelafigue Foundation and was honored to serve as the first lecturer of the Foundation's Lecture Series. He has served as the coordinator of the Governor-appointed Louisiana Historical Records Advisory Board and ex-officio member of the FRIENDS of the Louisiana State Archives Board.

Hardy has served on the following Museum Boards under the auspices of the Secretary of State: Caddo-Pine Island Oil Museum; E. D. White Historic Site, LA State Cotton Museum; Old State Capitol Advisory Board; Shreveport Water Works Museum; and The Louisiana Military Hall of Fame Museum.

Hardy authored A Brief History of the University of Southwestern Louisiana, 1900-1960 (Baton Rouge, Claitor's Publishing Division, 1973, reprinted in 2012, 2016, 2019, and 2023). Other noted publications appear in the Quebec Archives Quarterly, the LSU KAPPAN Contact, the Louisiana Education Research Journal, and The Boardman. Hardy's centerpiece article in the Society of American Archivists January/February 2014 *Archival Outlook* issue is entitled "Trademarks of a Vitally Functioning State Archives." He has been featured on C-SPAN and the History Channel.

Under Hardy's direction, the Louisiana State Archives, *Louisiana's Primary Governmental Records Repository*, received the prestigious Education Award in 2011 presented by the *Louisiana Trust* for HISTORIC PRESERVATION for its exhibits, "A Long, Long Time Ago" which recognized the contributions of the Long family, and the "West Florida Republic" which involved the participation of the eight parishes which were part of the seventy-four-day Republic.

Also under Hardy's leadership, the Louisiana State Archives was voted one of the hidden gems of the state's art community by *Southern Living Magazine*, and is listed as one of the 101 Best Web Sites for Genealogy by the *Family Tree Magazine*. The Louisiana State Archives is a partner in the *Multi-State Preservation Consortium* which offers a centralized, cost-effective interstate regional repository for state and local digital information, and has been featured in the National Geographic Society's United States Gulf Coast States Geotourism *MapGuide*.

Dr. Hardy was named one of USL's Outstanding Alumnus, Class of 1972, College of Education, and was honored to be featured in the Fall 2013 Alumni Association Section of *La LOUISIANE*, the University of Louisiana at Lafayette's Alumni Magazine.

Dr. Hardy was selected as the Louisiana Association of Museums' 2014 PUBLIC OFFICIAL OF THE YEAR as the individual who has demonstrated special or sustained, significant support of Louisiana's museums and historic sites. Under Dr. Hardy's leadership, Louisiana State Archives was awarded the 2016 Lt. Governor's *Preservationist Leadership Award*.

FOOTNOTES

CHAPTER 1

[1]Rodney Cline, *Builders of Louisiana Education*, (Baton Rouge: Bureau of Educational Materials and Research, College of Education, Louisiana State University, 1963), p. 27.

[2]Minns Sledge Robertson, *Public Education in Louisiana After 1898*(Baton Rouge: Bureau of Educational Materials and Research, 1952),pp. 9-10, quoting *Biennial Report of the State Superintendent of Public Education, 1898-1899*, (Baton Rouge: The Advocate, Official Journal of the State of Louisiana, 1900), pp. 4-5.

[3]Edwin L. Stephens, "Education in Louisiana in the Closing Decades of the Nineteenth Century." *Louisiana Historical Quarterly*, XVI (January-October, 1933), p. 55.

[4]John W. Faulk, "The History of Education in Lafayette Parish, Louisiana," (unpublished Master's thesis, Department of Elementary Education, Louisiana State University, 1933), chap, IV, p. 3.

[5]Edwin Lewis Stephens, "The Story of Acadian Education in Louisiana," *Louisiana Historical Quarterly,* XVIII, (April, 1935), p. 400.

[6]Margaret Stephens Jochem, "A History of Southwestern Louisiana Institute, 1900-1936" (unpublished Master's thesis, School of Education, George Peabody College for Teachers, 1937), p. 2.

[7]*Ibid.*

[8]Louisiana Legislature, Calendar of the House of Representatives of the State of Louisiana, Session of 1896, in the *Official Journal of the Proceedings of the House of Representatives of the State of Louisiana at the First Regular Session of the Fifth General Assembly,*(Baton Rouge: Advocate, 1896), p. 120.

[9]Stephens, "Acadian Education," *Louisiana Historical Quarterly,* XVIII, p. 402.

[10]Louisiana Legislature, Calendar of the Senate of the State of Louisiana in the *Official Journal of the Proceedings of the Senate of the State of Louisiana at the Second Regular Session Begun and Held in the City of Baton Rouge, May 16, 1898,* (Baton Rouge: Advocate, 1898), p. 6. See Appendix *p. 133* for the complete law creating the Institute.

[11]Pamphlet, A Statement of the Reasons Why Southwest Louisiana Industrial Institute Should be Located at Lafayette in the Parish of Lafayette, Submitted for the Consideration of the Board of trustees by the People, Lafayette, Louisiana, January, 1900, in University of Southwestern Louisiana Papers, Scrapbook, Vol. I, Southwestern Archives and Manuscripts Collection. Cited hereafter as USL Papers, S.A.M.C.

[12]Committee from New Iberia: C. C. Kramer, Water J. Burke, J. B. Lawton and C. Pierson.

FOOTNOTES

[13]Poster, A Brief, Setting Forth New Iberia's Claim for the Location of the Southwestern Louisiana Industrial Institute, in U.S.L. Papers, Scrapbook, Vol. I, S.A.M.C.

[14]Letter to the Citizens of the Parish of Lafayette from Alcide Judice, September 27, 1899, in U.S.L. Papers, Scrapbook, Vol. I. S.A.M.C.

[15]Clipping, "Industrial Institute; Directors of Southwestern Board Organize," n.d., in U.S.L. Papers, Scrapbook, Vol. I. S.A.M.C.

[16]Minutes, Executive Session of Board of Trustees, January 5, 1900, in U.S.L. Papers, Presidential Papers, S.A.M.C. See Appendix *p. 136* for private donors of Lafayette to S.L.I.I. Members of the first Board of Trustees were Governor Murphy Foster, President; Robert Martin, Vice President; Professor Brown Ayres, Secretary; Albert Estopinial, Captain John C. Buchanan, Mayor Jordan G. Lee, Dr. James A. Lee, and Thomas H. Lewis.

[17]Clipping, "The Southwestern Louisiana Industrial Institute," New Orleans *Daily States*, September 1, 1901, in U.S.L. Papers, Scrapbook, Vol. I, S.A.M.C.

[18]Extracts of the Address of Governor Murphy J. Foster, May 15, 1900, in U.S.L. Papers, Presidential Papers, S.A.M.C.

[19]Letter, Edwin L. Stephens to Crow Girard, January 6, 1900, in U.S.L. Papers, Presidential Papers, S.A.M.C. For Southwestern campus expansion see Appendix *p. 137.*

[20]Clipping, "Most Eventful Day in Lafayette's History," June 21, 1900, in U.S.L. Papers, Scrapbook, Vol. I, S.A.M.C.

[21]*First Biennial Report of the Southwestern Louisiana Industrial Institute, Lafayette, Louisiana* (New Orleans: The L. Graham C. Ltd., 1902), p. 13, in U.S.L. Papers, Scrapbook, Vol. I, S.A.M.C. The first faculty of the Institute were: Victor Leander Roy, Ashby Woodson, Miss Gertrude Mayfield, Miss Beverly Randolph, Miss Edith G. Dupre, Florent Sontag, L. W. Mayer, Mrs. Elizabeth Fowles Baker. See Appendix *p. 138* for positions of Southwestern's first faculty prior to their appointment to S.L.I.I.

[22]Letter, Edwin L. Stephens to Governor Murphy J. Foster, April 24, 1900, in U.S.L. Papers, Presidential Papers, S.A.M.C.

[23]Clipping, "Southwestern Louisiana Industrial Institute," n.d., in U.S.L. Papers, Scrapbook, Vol. I, S.A.M.C.

[24]*The Catalog of the Southwestern Industrial Institute*, 1903-1904, (New Orleans: The L. Graham Co., Ltd., 1902), p. 7.

[25]*Catalog*, 1902-1903, p. 6.

[26]*Ibid.*, p. 15.

[27]Editorial, "Lower Requirement Wanted," *Lafayette Advertiser*, in U.S.L. Papers, Presidential Papers, S.A.M.C.

[28]Letter, Edwin L. Stephens to Editor of Lafayette *Advertiser*, November 19, 1903, in U.S.L. Papers, Presidential Papers, S.A.M.C.

[29]Renamed Martin Hall. Renamed Foster Hall. Renamed Brown Ayres Hall.

[30]Clipping, "Industrial Institute; Dedication Exercises of the Institute Held Last Saturday—A Large Crowd Present," *The Lafayette Gazette*,

June 22, 1901, p. 17, in U.S.L. Papers, Scrapbook, Vol. I, S.A.M.C.
[31]Clipping, n.d., in U.S.L. Papers, Presidential Papers, S.A.M.C.
[32]*First Biennial Report*, p. 7, U.S.L. Papers, Scrapbook, Vol. I, S.A.M.C.
[33]*Ibid.*
[34]Undated. Memo, Beginning of the First Session, in U.S.L. Papers, Presidential Papers, S.A.M.C.
[35]*First Biennial Report*, p. 8, in U.S.L. Papers, Scrapbook, Vol. I, S.A.M.C.
[36] Clipping, "Activity Among the Southern Colleges," May 23, 1902, in U.S.L. Papers, Scrapbook, Vol. I, S.A.M.C.
[37]Alphabetical List of Students, in U.S.L. Papers, Student Life, S.A.M.C.
[38]*First Biennial Report*, p. 9, in U.S.L. Papers, Scrapbook, Vol. I, S.A.M.C. Other schools similar to S.L.I.I. at this time were LSU; Louisiana Normal, Natchitoches; and LII, Ruston.
[39]Petition of Southwestern Louisiana Industrial Students to Edwin L. Stephens, November 1902, in U.S.L. Papers, Presidential Papers, S.A.M.C.
[40]Letter, Edwin L. Stephens to J.L. Westbrook, February 24, 1903, in U.S.L. Papers, Presidential Papers, S.A.M.C.
[41]Clipping, "Lafayette's Greatest School," *The Crowley Signal*, February, 1904, in U.S.L. Papers, Presidential Papers, S.A.M.C.
[42] *Catalog*, 1903-1904, p. 33.
[43] *Catalog*, 1902-1903, pp. 33-34.
[44]Clipping, "Southwestern Louisiana Industrial Institute; Commencement Exercises," *The Lafayette Gazette*, May 30, 1903, in U.S.L. Papers, S.A.M.C. Special rate tickets for the Southern Pacific Railroad were provided by the Institute to all interested persons from Southwest Louisiana. Ten students comprised the first graduating class of the Institute.
[45]Letter, Edwin L. Stephens to Governor William W. Heard, December 6, 1903, in U.S.L. Papers, Presidential Papers, S.A.M.C. Members of the graduating class of 1903 were Annie T. Bell, Maxim A. Beraud, Rhena Boudreaux, Harold Demanade, Jacques Domengeaux, Alma L. Gulley, William Parkerson Mills, Henry De Koven Smedes, Edith Trahan, and Pothier J. Voorhies. The Lafayette *Gazette*, "Southwestern Louisiana Industrial Institute," May 30, 1903.
[46]Second Biennial Report of the Southwestern Louisiana Industrial Institute, p. 5, in U.S.L. Papers, Presidential Papers, S.A.M.C.
[47]*Ibid.*, p. 6.
[48]Edwin Lewis Stephens' Autobiographical Sketch; Sketch of My Career from the time of leaving Marshalltown Iowa, September 30, 1889, to enter Louisiana State University, Baton Rouge, in U.S.L. Papers, Presidential Papers, S.A.M.C.
[49]Clipping, "New Course of Study, Department of Telegraphy Established at the Southwestern Louisiana Industrial Institute at

Lafayette," January 1904, in U.S.L. Papers, Presidential Papers, S.A.M.C.

[50]*Catalog*, 1904-1905, p. 32.

[51]*Constitution and By-Laws of the Southwestern Louisiana Industrial Institute Alumni Association, Lafayette, Louisiana, 1904-1905,* (Lafayette: Lafayette Advertiser, 1905), pp. 1-3.

[52]*Ibid.*

[53]Clipping, "Southwestern Louisiana High School Notes," in U.S.L. Papers, Scrapbook, Vol. V, S.A.M.C. Original members of IAOA were Lake Charles, Welsh, Jennings, Crowley, Rayne, Opelousas, Breaux Bridge, St. Martinville, Abbeville, New Iberia, Jeanerette, Franklin, Patterson, and Morgan City High Schools. "Charter and By-Laws of the Interscholastic and Oratorical Association of Southwest Louisiana, 1904."

[54]Charter and By-Laws of the Interscholastic Athletic and Oratorical Association of Southwest Louisiana, Organized 1904, in U.S.L. Papers, Scrapbook, Vol. I, S.A.M.C.

[55]Letter, Edwin L. Stephens to Lieut. Col. Henry P. McCain, March 7, 1904, in U.S.L. Papers, Presidential Papers, S.A.M.C.

[56]Clipping, "Institute Cadets," March 25, 1905, in U.S.L. Papers, Scrapbook, Vol. I, S.A.M.C.

[57]*Institute Bulletin*, 1904-1905, p. 9.

[58]Announcement of the Southwestern Louisiana Industrial Institute Commencement Exercises; Annual Inspection of Exhibits from the Industrial and Manual Departments, Saturday, May 21, 1904, in U.S.L. Papers, Scrapbook, Vol. I, S.A.M.C.

[59]Clipping, "Industrial Institute; Fourth Annual Session Begins With Large Attendance," *Lafayette Gazette*, September 24, 1904, in U.S.L. Papers, Scrapbook, Vol. I, S.A.M.C.

[60]*Catalog* 1905-1906, pp. 48-53.

[61]Letter, Edwin L. Stephens to Dr. R. G. Hawkins, July 18, 1904, in U.S.L. Papers, Student Life, S.A.M.C. Foster Hall then became a boy's dormitory and DeClouet Hall was the new girl's dormitory.

[62]School Regulations, November 4, 1904, in U.S.L. Papers, Presidential Papers, S.A.M.C.

[63]Letter, Edwin L. Stephens to Dr. W.A. Poche, December 22, 1904, in U.S.L. Papers, Student Life, S.A.M.C.

[64]Letter, Edwin L. Stephens to Mr. E.M. Scott, January 26, 1905, in U.S.L. Papers, Student Life, S.A.M.C.

[65]Letter, Edwin L. Stephens to Mr. Theodore Strain, October 5, 1904, in U.S.L. Papers, Student Life, S.A.M.C.

[66]Letter, Edwin L. Stephens to Mr. E. Lafleur, March 21, 1905, in U.S.L. Papers, Student Life, S.A.M.C.

[67]Letter, Edwin L. Stephens to Mr. M. Talbot, March 26, 1905, in U.S.L. Papers, Student Life, S.A.M.C.

[68]*Institute Bulletin*, 1904-1905, p. 5.

[69]An Invitation to the Graduation Exercises of May 28-29, 1905, in U.S.L. Papers, Scrapbook, Vol. I, S.A.M.C.
[70]Letter, Edwin L. Stephens to Thomas H. Harris, June 29, 1912, in U.S.L. Papers, Student Life, S.A.M.C. Academic-Industrial, 21; Manual Training, 4; Commercial, 21; Stenography, 7; Home Economics, 9.

CHAPTER II

[1]Edwin Lewis Stephens Papers, (Film 232 Documents and Artifacts: This film consists of papers, addresses, and speeches), 1872-1938, and Florence Kennedy, "Edwin Lewis Stephens' Influence on Education" (unpublished research paper, 1953), pp. 1-3.
[2]Mrs. Ora Michael Childress, "Edwin Lewis Stephens Scholar and Educator," (unpublished paper presented to Stephens Memorial Library, 193?), pp. 26-27. This $5,000 scholarship was established by Helen Miller Gould in memory of her father, Jay Gould.
[3]Mrs. Margaret Stephens, "The Life Story of Edwin Lewis Stephens," *The Southwestern Louisiana Journal,* IV January, 1960, p. 19. This thesis included a history of public education in Louisiana (1945-1899), the organization and administration of Louisiana's public education, and the quality of Louisiana teachers and the courses taught. A comparison of Louisiana education is made to national standards, and a conclusion is reached which advocated one organized state educational system where administrative decisions are made mostly through state supervision instead of the existing system where parishes varied in educational programs.
[4]Childress, "Stephens," pp. 26-27.
[5]Edwin Lewis Stephens Papers, 1872-1938.
[6]*Ibid.*
[7]Clipping, "Re-election of President Stephens," New Orleans *States,* n.d., in U.S.L. Papers, Scrapbook, 1913-14, S.A.M.C.
[8]Clipping, "Dr. Stephens and Southwestern," The Lafayette *Gazette,* May 29, 1913, in U.S.L. Papers, Scrapbook, 1913-14, p. 2, S.A.M.C.
[9]Undated Poster, Final Report of the Red Cross Drive by Dr. Stephens to the Editor of the Lafayette *Advertiser,* in U.S.L. Papers, Scrapbook, 1917-18, p. 70, S.A.M.C.
[10]Edwin Lewis Stephens Papers, (Film 232: Documents and Artifacts), 1872-1938.
[11]*Ibid.*
[12]Letter, Edwin Lewis Stephens to the Editor of *The Daily Advertiser,* December 12, 1905, in U.S.L. Papers, Presidential Papers, 1905-07, S.A.M.C.
[13]Telephone Interview with Mrs. Ruth Mouton Hamilton, July 3, 1968, Lafayette, Louisiana.
[14]Clipping, "A Fine Louisiana School," The Crowley *Signal,* October, 1905, in U.S.L. Papers, Presidential Papers, 1910-11, S.A.M.C.
[15]Editorial, "Probably an Oversight," New Orleans *States,* June 21, 1910, in U.S.L. Papers, Presidential Papers, 1910-11, S.A.M.C.

[16]Clipping, "The Public," Cited as Chicago newspaper in Scrapbook, August 26, 1905, in U.S.L. Papers, Scrapbook, 1899-1907, p. 107, S.A.M.C.

[17]Memorandum, October 2, 1914, in U.S.L. Papers, Scrapbook, 1908-24, p. 7, S.A.M.C.

[18]Institute Bulletin, (IV, No. 4, June, 1908), in U.S.L. Papers, Scrapbook, 1908-24, p. 1. S.A.M.C.

[19]Letter, Edwin L. Stephens to Professor W. J. Avery, March 20, 1907, in U.S.L. Papers, Presidential Papers, 1905-07, S.A.M.C.

[20]Statement to the Board of Trustees of Southwestern by President Stephens, in U.S.L. Papers, Scrapbook, 1908-24, S.A.M.C.

[21]Letter, Edwin L. Stephens to [Dear Sir], August 11, 1910, in U.S.L. Papers, Presidential Papers, 1910, S.A.M.C.

[22]Memo, Southwestern Louisiana Industrial Institute, Lafayette, Louisiana, Announcements 1910-11 in U.S.L. Papers, Presidential Papers, 1910-11, S.A.M.C.

[23]Minutes, Committee on Classification, in U.S.L. Papers, Presidential Papers, 1910-11, S.A.M.C.

[24]Memo, Sixth Biennial Report of the Southwestern Industrial Institute, Lafayette, Louisiana, 1912, in U.S.L. Papers, Presidential Papers, 1912, S.A.M.C.

[25]Memo, Statement to the Board of Trustees of the Southwestern Louisiana Industrial Institute at the Annual Meeting of May 26, 1913, Regarding Standards of the Courses of Study and Expense to Students as Related to the Growth and Progress of the Institution, in U.S.L. Papers, Presidential Papers, 1913, S.A.M.C.

[26]Clipping, "Institute Begins New Session," n.n., n.d., in U.S.L. Papers, Scrapbook, 1915-16, S.A.M.C. The news article states that the session is 1916-1917.

[27]Memo, President Stephens' Statement, in U.S.L. Papers, Presidential Papers, 1917, S.A.M.C.

[28]Undated Memo, Announcements for 1920-1921, in U.S.L. Papers, Presidential Papers, 1920, S.A.M.C.

[29]Undated Memo, Victor L. Roy, Chemistry and Physics Instructor, in U.S.L. Papers, Presidential Papers, 1905-07, S.A.M.C.

[30]Clipping, "Government Demonstration Farm to be Established at Institute," n.n., September 18, 1907, in U.S.L. Papers, Scrapbook, 1899-1907, p. 151, S.A.M.C.

[31]Frederick Williamson, *Origin and Growth of Agricultural Extension in Louisiana—1860-1948; How it Opened the Road for Progress in Better Farming and Rural Living*, (Baton Rouge: Louisiana State University and Agricultural and Mechanical College, Division of Agricultural Extension, 1951), p. 46.

[32]Institute Bulletin, (IV, No. 2, December, 1907), in U.S.L. Papers, Presidential Papers, 1907-09, S.A.M.C.

[33]Williamson, *Origin and Growth*, p. 50.

[34]Memo, Jordan G. Lee, Jr., Agriculture, in U.S.L. Papers, in Student Life, 1909; and Address, Edwin L. Stephens to Members of the Board

of Trustees, December 23, 1909, in U.S.L. Papers, Presidential Papers, 1909, S.A.M.C. Lee Hall on the campus was named in honor of Mr. Jordan G. Lee, Jr.

[35]Clipping, "Industrial Institute; New Typewriters Received— Department of Telegraphy to Open About Dec. 1," The Lafayette *Advertiser*, November 1, 1907, in U.S.L. Papers, Scrapbook, 1899-1907, p. 153; and Institute Bulletin, October, 1908, in U.S.L. Papers, Scrapbook, 1908-24, S.A.M.C.

[36]*Seventh Biennial Report of the Southwestern Louisiana Industrial Institute*, Lafayette, Louisiana 1914, p. 10.

[37]Clipping, "Radio School Shows Progress," The Lafayette *Advertiser*, January 31, 1918; and "Radio Class Opens at Lafayette," n.n., n.d., in U.S.L. Papers, Scrapbook, 1908-24, p. 62, S.A.M.C. As a result of training in this course at Southwestern, the pay and rank of the inducted sailor increased.

[38]Letter, Edwin L. Stephens to Miss Emily Geneux, August 2, 1918, in U.S.L. Papers, Student Life, 1918, S.A.M.C.

[39]Manuscript, W. Elmer Brown, Commercial Department Reorganized, in U.S.L. Papers, Student Life, 1920, S.A.M.C.

[40]Clipping, "This is Last Week for Registration in the Night Classes of S.L.I. Commerce and Business Administration Dept.," February, 1924, n.n., in U.S.L. Papers, Scrapbook, 1924-26, p. 8, S.A.M.C. Trade unionism is similar to business management.

[41]Letter, Edwin L. Stephens to Mr. Warren Thomas, November 1, 1919, in U.S.L. Papers, Student Life, 1919; and clipping, "SLI Course in Advertising is to be Started," n.n., in U.S.L. Papers, Scrapbook, 1923-24, p. 22, S.A.M.C.

[42]Pamphlet, Fourth Biennial Report of Southwestern Louisiana Industrial Institute, in U.S.L. Papers, Scrapbook, 1908-24, p. 10, S.A.M.C.

[43]Clipping, "That Second Normal School," n.n., June 16, 1908, in U.S.L. Papers, Scrapbook, 1908-24, p. 10, S.A.M.C.

[44]Clipping, "The Latest News in All Louisiana; President Stephens Details the Dire Needs of the Industrial," *The Times Picayune*, May 24, 1906, in U.S.L. Papers, Scrapbook, 1899-1907, p. 119, S.A.M.C.

[45]Memo, Institute Notes, May 30, 1917, in U.S.L. Papers, Presidential papers, 1917, S.A.M.C.

[46]Memo, in U.S.L. Papers, Presidential Papers, 1909, S.A.M.C.

[47]Letter, Edwin L. Stephens to Mr. C. R. Couvillon, June 4, 1909, in U.S.L. Papers, Student Life, 1909, S.A.M.C.

[48]Memo to Louisiana Teachers and Superintendents, August 12, 1911, in U.S.L. Papers, Presidential Papers, 1910-11, S.A.M.C.

[49]Institute Bulletin, (IX, No. 1, May, 1912), in U.S.L. Papers, Student Life, 1912, S.A.M.C.

[50]Telegram, Edwin L. Stephens to the Honorable. The State Board of Education, July 29, 1912, in U.S.L. Papers, Presidential Papers, 1912, S.A.M.C.

[51]Memo, in U.S.L. Papers, n.n., n.d., Presidential Papers, 1912, S.A.M.C.

[52]Letter, Thomas Harris to Edwin Lewis Stephens, August 19, 1912, in U.S.L. Papers, Presidential Papers, 1912, S.A.M.C.

[53]House Bill No. 100, in U.S.L. Papers, Presidential Papers, 1914, S.A.M.C.

[54]Clippings, "Says Normal has Monopoly for Teachers," n.n., June 24, 1914; and "The Catechism of a Lost Cause; Dr. Stephens' Service as Lobbyist," n.n., n.d., in U.S.L. Papers, Presidential Papers, 194, and Scrapbook, 1913-14, p. 13, S.A.M.C.

[55]Letter, Thomas H. Harris to Edwin L. Stephens, May 6, 1915, in U.S.L. Papers, Presidential Papers, 1915, S.A.M.C.

[56]Letter, Edwin L. Stephens to Thomas H. Harris, August 19, 1916, in U.S.L. Papers, Presidential Papers, 1916, S.A.M.C.

[57]Memo, Institute Notes, May 30, 1917, in U.S.L. Papers, Presidential Papers, 1917, S.A.M.C.

CHAPTER III

[1]Letter, Edwin L. Stephens to Victor L. Roy, President of Louisiana State Normal College, May 19, 1926, in U.S.L. Papers, Presidential Papers, 1926, S.A.M.C.

[2]Memo, Announcements for 1920-21, in U.S.L. Papers, Presidential Papers, 1920; and Edwin L. Stephens to Mr. D. Sassone, September 23, 1921, in U.S.L. Papers, Student Life, 1921, S.A.M.C.

[3]Announcements for 1920-21, in U.S.L. Papers, Presidential Papers, 1920, S.A.M.C.

[4]Clipping, "South Louisiana Institute of Liberal and Technical Learning, Lafayette, Louisiana, Edwin L. Stephens, President," n.n., n.d., in U.S.L. Papers, Scrapbook, 1920-21, p. 103, S.A.M.C.

[5]Notice, Announcement of the Division of Extension, in U.S.L. Papers, Scrapbook, 1926-27, p. 118, S.A.M.C. This Division of Extension was similar to Night School.

[6]Clipping, "643 Registered in S.L.I. Mail Course," Summer 1928, n.n., in U.S.L. Papers, Scrapbook, 1927-28, p. 129, S.A.M.C.

[7]Minutes of the Meeting of the Louisiana State Board of Education held in Baton Rouge, January 8, 1923, in U.S.L. Papers, Presidential Papers, 1923, S.A.M.C.

[8]Clipping, "School Receipts Found $3,185,607 Higher this Year," in U.S.L. Papers, Scrapbook, 1923-24, p. 19, S.A.M.C.

[9]Clipping, "Dr. E. L. Stephens Issues Statement in Regard to the Threatened Charges Against Him by Local Board Member," n.n., n.d., in U.S.L. Papers, Scrapbook, 1923-24, p. 19, S.A.M.C.

[10]Clipping, "State Board of Education Declares Southwestern 'Is in an Excellent Condition,'" n.n., n.d., in U.S.L. Papers, Scrapbook, 1923-24, p. 154, S.A.M.C.

[11]*Ibid.*

[12]Clippings, "Charges Not Filed Against Dr. Stephens," n.n., November 22, 1923; and "Education Board Clears Stephens Rebukes Mouton," in U.S.L. Papers, Scrapbook, 1923-24, p. 20, S.A.M.C.

[13]Clipping, "Dr. E. L. Stephens and Fernand Mouton in Encounter," *The Daily Advertiser* April 14, 1926, in U.S.L. Papers, Scrapbook, 1926-27, p. 40, S.A.M.C.

[14]Clipping, "Faculty of SLI Urges Support for Dr. E. L. Stephens," n.n., September, 1926, in U.S.L. Papers, Scrapbook, 1926-27, p. 44, S.A.M.C.

[15]Clipping, "Students Score Mouton, Uphold Institute's Head," n.n., April 16, 1926, in U.S.L. Papers, Scrapbook, 1926-27, p. 44, S.A.M.C.

[16]Clippings, "Re-Election of Dr. Stephens as S.L.I. Head is Asked in Resolution by Student Body;" "SLI Faculty, Staff Urge Re-Election of Dr. Stephens;" "Parent-Teacher Association Urges Dr. E. L. Stephens Be Reappointed as S.L.I. Head;" and "Southwestern Alumni Ask for Dr. Stephens' Reappointment," in U.S.L. Papers, Scrapbook, 1929-30, pp. 88-90, S.A.M.C.

[17]Clipping, "Dr. E. L. Stephens, Mentioned as New State University President Will Not Comment Definitely at this Time," *The Daily Advertiser*, n.d. in U.S.L. Papers, Scrapbook, 1923-24, p. 30. Thomas D. Boyd did not resign officially from LSU until 1926, S.A.M.C.

[18]Clipping, "Dr. Stephens is Urged as LSU Head," n.n., n.d., in U.S.L. Papers, 1926-27, p. 117. Thomas W. Atkinson, Dean of the LSU College of Engineering, replaced by Boyd in 1927, S.A.M.C.

[19]Clipping, "Southwestern is Recognized Standard College by the Southern Association Today," *The Daily Advertiser*, Fall 1925, in U.S.L. Papers, Scrapbook, 1924-26, p. 181, S.A.M.C.

[20]Clipping, "Achievement of S.L.I. in Reaching High Goal is Told by Dr. E.L. Stephens," Fall 1925, in U.S.L. Papers, Scrapbook, 1924-26, p. 182, S.A.M.C.

[21]Loma Knighten, "A History of the Library of Southwestern Louisiana Institute 1900-1948," unpublished Master thesis, Columbia University, 1949), p. 12-19.

[22]*L'Acadien*, 1914; Resolution Adopted by the Faculty of the Southwestern Louisiana Industrial Institute, January 1, 1912, in U.S.L. Papers, Presidential Papers, 1912, S.A.M.C.

[23]Knighten "A History of the Library," p. 25.

[24]Announcement, Donation of Southwestern Institute Library, May 10, 1924, in U.S.L. Papers, Presidential Papers, 1924, S.A.M.C.

[25]Clipping, "Library Reach a Total of 8,000," n.n., Spring 1925, in U.S.L. Papers, Scrapbook, 1924-26, p. 182, S.A.M.C. Interview with Miss Pearl Segura, June 14, 1968, Lafayette, Louisiana.

[26]Clipping, "Library Study of SLI List," n.n., n.d., in U.S.L. Papers, Scrapbook, 1930-31, p. 25, S.A.M.C.

[27]Undated Memo, Southwestern Louisiana Institute, in U.S.L. Papers, Presidential Papers, 1931, S.A.M.C.

[28]Letter, Fenner W. Smith to *[Dear Classmates]* May 15, 1937, in U.S.L. Papers, Presidential Papers, 1937, S.A.M.C.

FOOTNOTES

[29]Florence Kennedy, "Edwin Lewis Stephens' Influence on Education" (unpublished research paper, 1953), p. 8.

[30]Address, Edwin L. Stephens to the President and Members, Louisiana State Board of Education, January 1, 1938, in U.S.L. Papers, Presidential Papers, 1938, S.A.M.C.

[31]Interview with James Stewart Bonnet, May 24, 1968, Lafayette, Louisiana; and Interview with Robert Angelle, May 25, 1968, Cecilia, Louisiana.

[32]Interview with A. Wilmot Dalferes, July 9, 1968, Lafayette, Louisiana.

[33]Interview with Joel Lafayette Fletcher, June 14, 1968, Lafayette, Louisiana.

[34]Undated Memo, in U.S.L. Papers, Presidential Papers, 1938, S.A.M.C.

[35]Joel Lafayette Fletcher, "The First President – Edwin Lewis Stephens," Lafayette, Louisiana, 1950, p. [2].

CHAPTER IV

[1]Allan P. Sindler, *Huey Long's Louisiana: State Politics, 1920-1952*, Baltimore: John Hopkins Press, 1956, p. 83.

[2]*Ibid.*, p. 86.

[3]*Ibid.*, p. 126.

[4]Clipping, "Lether Frazar Dies in Hospital," *The Times Picayune*, May 16, 1960, p. 1.

[5]Clippings, "Frazar Funeral Rites Scheduled in Lake Charles," *The Daily Advertiser*, May 16, 1960, p. 1; and "Dr. E. L. Stephens, Head of S.L.I., Retires," n.n., January 3, 1938, in U.S.L. Papers, Scrapbook, 1937-38, p. 38, S.A.M.C.

[6]Southwestern Louisiana Institute, *Faculty Biographical Sketches*, September 16, 1940, p. 5. Act No. 83, House of Bill No. 127, 1936.

[7]Clipping, "Dr. E. L. Stephens Retired Monday," *The Vermilion*, January 7, 1938, p. 1.

[8]Interview with James Stewart Bonnet, May 24, 1968, Lafayette, Louisiana; and Interview with Joseph Riehl, June 19, 1968, Lafayette, Louisiana.

[9]Editorial, "Historical Epoch Closes," *The Daily Advertiser*, January 3, 1938, in U.S.L. Papers, Scrapbook, 1937-38, p. 34, S.A.M.C.

[10]Interview with Dr. Kenneth B. Hait, May 23, 1968.

[11]Clipping, "Needs of S.L.I. Told to Alumni," The Beaumont *Enterprise*, March 3, 1939, in U.S.L. Papers, Scrapbook, 1937-38, p. 79, S.A.M.C.

[12]Clippings, "New Dormitories for Southwestern," Monroe *News-Star*, May 5, 1938; and "Student Center at S.L.I. to be Named for Business Head," The Beaumont *Enterprise*, May 30, 1938, in U.S.L. Papers, Scrapbook, 1938, pp. 6, 12, S.A.M.C. Atwood William Bittle had been S.L.I.'s Business Manager Since 1922.

[13]Clippings, "Plan Complete Dormitory at S.L.I. by Fall," *The Daily Advertiser*, July 7, 1922; and "Lowest Dormitory Bid is $169,313.12,"

The Times Picayune, July 13, 1938, in U.S.L. Papers, Scrapbook, 1938, p. 33, 28, S.A.M.C.
[14]Clipping, "S.L.I. President Plans Fight for More Facilities," *The Times Picayune*, April 1, 1938, in U.S.L. Papers, Scrapbook, 1937-38, p. 109, S.A.M.C.
[15]Interview with James Stewart Bonnet, May 24, 1968, Lafayette, Louisiana.
[16]*Ibid.* PWA funds were grant-type appropriations used at Southwestern primarily for building construction and covered walks.
[17]Clipping, "S.L.I. Building Program Aided by PWA Grants," *The Times Picayune*, September 9, 1938, in U.S.L. Papers, Scrapbook, 1938, p. 54, S.A.M.C.
[18]Clippings, "Lether Frazar Ends First Year as Head of S.L.I.," The Beaumont *Enterprise*, January 1, 1939, in U.S.L. Papers, Scrapbook, 1938-39; and "S.L.I. Moving Forward Under Administration of L.E. Frazar," *The Daily Advertiser*, January 4, 1939, in U.S.L. Papers, Scrapbook, 1939, p. 45, S.A.M.C. These buildings included:

Girl's Dormitory	$ 82,000
Girl's Dormitory	81,000
Fine Arts Building	338,000
Clinic and Infirmary	75,000
Elementary Junior School	173,000
Library Building	221,000
Additions to Dining Hall	24,000
President's Residence	27,000
Stadium Dormitory	185,000
Industrial Arts Building	93,000
Girl's Gymnasium	82,000
Demonstration High School	117,000
Engineering Building and Laboratory	132,000
Miscellaneous items: Services, walks, landscaping, physical education, tennis courts, repairs, alterations	183,000
Architectural Fees	188,741
Total	$2,001,741

[19]Clipping, "Hall Will Honor Dr. E. L. Stephens," *The Times Picayune*, February 25, 1939, in U.S.L. Papers, Scrapbook, 1938-39, S.A.M.C.
[20]Clipping, "Name Academy Buildings S.L.I. Mouton Hall," *The Daily Advertiser*, May 6, 1940, in U.S.L. Papers, Scrapbook, 1940, S.A.M.C. Named for Alexander Mouton, ninth governor of Louisiana, and the late Julian Mouton, former member of the Circuit Court of Appeals.
[21]Clipping, "Buildings Under Construction at Southwestern," The Lafayette *Progress*, July 28, 1939, in U.S.L. Papers, Scrapbook, 1939, p. 45, S.A.M.C. The reason for the later change in the names of the buildings is House Bill No. 5 in 1940 introduced by Mr. Frank M. Bacque, Representative of Lafayette Parish which read, "Making it

unlawful to name in honor of any living person any public building…That in all cases where such public buildings…" have been so named "to change the name of said building…and to cause to be destroyed, defaced or removed from said building, all plaques, signs or other evidence of the old name that may appear thereon…"
[22]Clipping, "To Name S.L.I. Building After Late Dr. Saucier," *The Daily Advertiser,* March 2, 1940, in U.S.L. Papers, Scrapbook, 1939-40, S.A.M.C.
[23]Clipping, "Extend Invitation to Open House at S.L.I. Library Tuesday, *The Daily Advertiser*, January 6, 1940; and "Classes Held in New S.L.I. Building," The Beaumont *Enterprise*, February 2, 1940, in U.S.L. Papers, Scrapbook, 1939-40, S.A.M.C.
[24]Clippings, "S.L.I. Student Divisions Given," *The Times Picayune*, October 18, 1938, in U.S.L. Papers, Scrapbook, 1938, p. 86; and "2308 registered for S.L.I. Study," *The Times Picayune*, September 21, 1940, Scrapbook, 1940, S.A.M.C. Southwestern's enrollment 1938-39: 1,867; 1940-41: 2,308.
[25]Clipping, "Additional Bus for Commuters to S.L.I.," *The Daily Advertiser,* August 23, 1938, in U.S.L. Papers, Scrapbook, 1938, p. 45, S.A.M.C.
[26]Southwestern Louisiana *Catalog*, 1937-38, pp. 10-26; 1938-39, pp. 12-18; 1940-41, p. 16.
[27]Clipping, "G. W. Barth Named Head Newly Created Music Dept. S.L.I.," *The Daily Advertiser*, July 6, 1938, in U.S.L. Papers, Scrapbook, 1938, p. 26, S.A.M.C.
[28]*Catalog*, 1939-40, p. 95.
[29]Clipping, "Three New Fields Offered to Students Who Attend S.L.I.," The Lafayette *Progress,* October 1, 1940, in U.S.L. Papers, Scrapbook, 1940, S.A.M.C.
[30]Clipping, "Film Library is Installed at Southwestern," *The Daily Advertiser*, March 8, 1940, in U.S.L. Papers, Scrapbook, 1940, S.A.M.C.
[31]Clipping "Plane Mechanics to be Taught at Southwestern," *The Daily Advertiser*, September 29, 1939, in U.S.L. Papers, Scrapbook, 1939, S.A.M.C.
[32]Clippings, "Dance Course to be Offered at Southwestern," *The Daily Advertiser*, August 16, 1939, in U.S.L. Papers, Scrapbook, 1939, p. 58, S.A.M.C.
[33]Clipping, "Journalism Course to be Offered at S.L.I.," The Beaumont *Enterprise*, July 7, 1939, in U.S.L. Papers, Scrapbook, 1939, p. 39, S.A.M.C.
[34]Clipping, "Plan Create Engineering School S.L.I.," *The Daily Advertiser*, July 7, 1939, in U.S.L. Papers, Scrapbook, 1939, S.A.M.C.
[35]Clipping, "New Deans Named at S.L.I.," n.n., January 30, 1938, in U.S.L. Papers, Scrapbook, 1937-38, p. 56, S.A.M.C.
[36]Clipping, "Engineering Unit Planned at S.L.I.," *The Times Picayune,* July 27, 1939, in U.S.L. Papers, Scrapbook, 1939, p.43, S.A.M.C.

[37]Clipping, "Harris Proposes S.L.I. be Made a Graduate School," *The Times Picayune*, July 13, 1939, in U.S.L. Papers, Scrapbook, 1939, p. 28, S.A.M.C.

[38]Clipping, "L. E. Frazar Named to Succeed Abernathy as Highway Head," n.n., July 18, 1939, in U.S.L. Papers, Scrapbook, 1939, p. 33, S.A.M.C.

[39]*Ibid.*

[40]Clipping, "L. E. Frazar Resigns Post as head of Highway Commission," n.n., July 24, 1939, in U.S.L. Papers, Scrapbook, 1939, p. 40, S.A.M.C.; and Interview with James Stewart Bonnet, May 24, 1968, Lafayette, Louisiana.

[41]Clipping, "Lether E. Frazar Resigns as President of Southwestern," *The Daily Advertiser*, August 2, 1940, in U.S.L. Papers, Scrapbook, 1940, S.A.M.C.

[42]Interview with James Stewart Bonnet, May 24, 1968, Lafayette, Louisiana.

[43]Interview with Robert Angelle, May 25, 1968, Cecilia, Louisiana.

[44]Robert Cook and Eleanor Carrol, eds., *Trustees and Presidents of American Colleges and Universities, 1955-56*, (Nashville, Tenn.: Who's Who in American Education, Inc., 1955), p. 87.

[45]Edwin Adams Davis, *The Story of Louisiana*, Vol. I (New Orelans: J. F. Hyer Publishing Co., 1960), p. 347.

[46]Clipping, "Lether Frazar Dies in Hospital," *The Times Picayune*, May 16, 1960, p. 1.

[47]See Appendix *p. 140* for major construction on Southwestern's campus up to 1938.

CHAPTER V

[1]Kenneth Lewis Weber, "Joel Lafayette Fletcher: Distinguished Educator and Outstanding American," 1967, in Joel L. Fletcher Papers, S.A.M.C.; and Clipping, "New Deans Named at SLI," n.n., January 30, 1938, in U.S.L. Papers, Scrapbook, 1937-38, p. 56, S.A.M.C. Interview with Joel Lafayette Fletcher, March 20, 1969, Lafayette, Louisiana.

[2]*Ibid.*

[3]Interview with Joel Lafayette Fletcher, June 14, 1968, Lafayette, Louisiana.

[4]Weber, "Joel L. Fletcher," S.A.M.C.

[5]Interview with Joseph A. Riehl, June 19, 1968, Lafayette, Louisiana.

[6]Clipping, "J. L. Fletcher is Recommended for S.L.I. Post," *The Daily Advertiser*, October 19, 1940; and "Joel L. Fletcher is Appointed President of Southwestern," *The Daily Advertiser*, November 15, 1940, in U.S.L. Papers, Scrapbook, 1940, S.A.M.C.

[7]Clipping, "J. L. Fletcher Takes Over the Presidency of S.L.I. Wednesday," *The Daily Advertiser*, January 2, 1941, in U.S.L. Papers, Scrapbook, 1940-41.

[8]Harris E. Starr, ed., *Dictionary of American Biography*, Vol. 21, pp. 21-22.

[9]Joel L. Fletcher, "Education—The Right of Every Human Being," in "Louisiana Education," Vol. 1, No. 8, S.A.M.C.

[10]Fletcher, "Fundamental of Survival is Knowledge," in "Louisiana Education," Vol. 2, No. 95, S.A.M.C.

[11]Fletcher, "Education—The Indispensable Asset for Your Child," in "Louisiana Education," Vol. 1, No. 30, S.A.M.C.

[12]This enabled young men from low-income families to attend Southwestern by working on the farm to pay for tuition and some expenses.

[13]Fletcher, "Louisiana Education," Vol. 1, No. 8, S.A.M.C.

[14]Clipping, "Dr. Arceneaux is named S.L.I. Dean of Agriculture," *The Times Picayune*, January 27, 1941, in U.S.L. Papers, Scrapbook, 1940-41, S.A.M.C. Interview with Joel L. Fletcher, March 20, 1969, Lafayette, Louisiana.

[15]Clipping, "New Program Being Planned at Southwestern," *The Daily Advertiser*, December 8, 1941, in U.S.L. Papers, Scrapbook, 1941-42, S.A.M.C.

[16]Clipping, "No More Standing in Lines at SLI for Registration," *The Daily Iberian*, May 24, 1946, in U.S.L. Papers, Scrapbook, 1940-41, S.A.M.C.

[17]Clipping, "S.L.I. Given Back Its Standing by Southern Group," *The Times Picayune*, December 20, 1941, in U.S.L. Papers, Scrapbook, 1940-41, S.A.M.C.

[18]Clipping, "S.L.I. Gets Fund for Equipment in Defense Work," *The Times Picayune*, July 20, 1941, in U.S.L. Papers, Scrapbook, 1941, S.A.M.C.

[19]*Catalog*, 1943-44, pp. 26-27.

[20]*Catalog*, 1945-46, pp. 27-28.

[21]Telephone interview with James Stewart Bonnet, August 20, 1968, Lafayette, Louisiana.

[22]Clipping, "Southwestern Bids Farewell to V-12 Unit with dance," *The Vermilion*, October 12, 1945.

[23]Clipping, "Southwestern Commended by the U.S. Navy," *The Daily Advertiser*, October 15, 1945.

[24]Clipping, "Newly Organized Veterans' Club Plans Active Program at SLI," *The Vermilion*, November 30, 1945.

[25]Clipping, "Vets Bring SLI Campus Unique Accent," *The Daily Advertiser*, September 17, 1950.

[26]Clipping, "Vets Population at SLI Drop to 33%," *The Vermilion*, December 9, 1949.

[27]Clipping, "R. L. Browne Appointed to Head Newly Organized P.E. Department," *The Vermilion*, December 7, 1945.

[28]Clipping, "S.L.I. Now Largest State College," *The Vermilion*, October 11, 1946.

[29]Announcement, History of SLI, 1952, in U.S.L. Papers, Presidential Papers, 1900-58, S.A.M.C

[30]*Catalog*, 1956-57, p. 27.

[31]Clipping, "Campus Streets are Named In Honor of Faculty Members," *The Vermilion*, July 21, 1950.

[32]*Catalog*, 1955-56, p. 25.

[33]Telephone interview with Helen A. Meyer, August 20, 1968, Lafayette, Louisiana.

[34]*Catalog*, 1953-43, p. 126.

[35]*Catalog*, 1956-57, p. 27.

[36]*Catalog*, 1953-54, p. 129.

[37]Clipping, "School of Home Economics Formed," *The Vermilion*, October 23, 1953.

[38]Clipping, "New PBX Near Completion; $25,000 Telephone Exchange May Be Completed by Monday," *The Vermilion*, January 9, 1953.

[39]Clipping, "'Electronic Brain' Machine Now in Operation at SLI," *The Vermilion*, September 24, 1954.

[40]Clipping, "Summer Registration for First Time at Coliseum; New IBM Method Used," *The Vermilion*, June 10, 1960.

[41]Clippings, "4 Negroes Seek Entrance to SLI," *The Daily Advertiser*, January 5, 1954; and "2 Federal Judges Named for SLI Segregation Suit," *The Daily Advertiser*, January 8, 1954.

[42]Clipping, "SLI Segregation Suit Under Advisement," *The Daily Advertiser*, February 21, 1954.

[43]Clipping, "Federal Judges Order SLI to Admit Negro Students; Court Ruling Equal Accommodations Not Available to Race in Area," *The Daily Advertiser*, April 23, 1954.

[44]Clipping, "SLI Negro Ruling Will Be Appealed," *The Daily Advertiser*, April 30, 1954.

[45]Clipping, "Segregation in Public Schools Struck Down by Supreme Court," *The Daily Advertiser*, May 17, 1954.

[46]Clipping, "Court Broadens Segregation Ban," *The Daily Advertiser*, May 24, 1954.

[47]Clipping, "Negro Woman Applies for SLI Summer Session," *The Daily Advertiser*, June 7, 1954.

[48]Clipping, "Judgement Final in SLI Suit by 4 Negroes," *The Daily Advertiser*, July 18, 1954.

[49]Clipping, "Negro Registers at SLI to Study in Engineering," *The Daily Advertiser*, July 22, 1954; and Telephone interview with Joseph Riehl, August 20, 1968; Lafayette, Louisiana.

[50]Announcement, Southwestern Louisiana Institute, Distribution of Students by Race Within the Several Academic Areas, in U.S.L. Papers, Presidential Papers, 1900-58, S.A.M.C.

[51]Office of the Registrar, University of Southwestern Louisiana.

[52]Clipping, "Pre-Med Tech School Receives Committee O.K.," *The Vermilion*, July 29, 1955.

[53]Clipping, "$5,000 First Gift to SLI Foundation," *The Vermilion*, October 7, 1955.

[54]Clipping, "Collection of 200 Books Given SLI Library by Former Southwesterner," The Lafayette *Progress*, April 1, 1948, in U.S.L. Papers, Scrapbook, 1948, S.A.M.C.

FOOTNOTES

FOOTNOTES

[55]Clipping, "Caffery Library is Donated to SLI," *The Vermilion,* November 11, 1949.

[56]*Catalog,* 1956-57, pp. 29-30.

[57]Clipping, "Stephens Ranks High in State Library Survey," *The Vermilion,* February 15, 1957.

[58]Clipping, "Campus Library Grows With SLI," *The Vermilion,* October 9, 1959.

[59]Named for Stafford M. Blackham, a native of Utah and past head of the Southwestern animal husbandry department.

[60]Dormitories named for Elizabeth Fowles Baker, Emily Hamilton Huger, and Beverly Randolph Stephens.

[61]Named for William A. Montgomery, Lafayette druggist and one-time member of the state legislature and state board of education.

[62]Clipping, Jim La Caffinie, "SLI Acquires Cultural Hall," *The Daily Advertiser,* February 20, 1955.

[63]Roy Hall was named for the Southwest Louisiana family of whom J. Arthur Roy served on Southwestern's Board of Trustees and later on the Executive Committee of the college. Caffery Hall was named for the southwest Louisiana family of whom Charles D. Caffery served on Southwestern's Board of Trustees during the early days of the college.

[64]Memorial Student Union Complex was named for Southwestern's dead in both World Wars. Coronna Hall was named for B. N. Coronna who contributed money to Southwestern during its formative years. Guillory and Olivier Halls were named for southwest Louisiana families.

[65]Resweber and Billeaud Halls were named for southwest Louisiana families. H. Flood Madison Hall was named for a former member and president of the state board of education.

[66]Clippings, "USL President Entering His 45th Year of Service to the University," *The Daily Advertiser,* August 2, 1964; "President Fletcher Will Begin 45th Year at USL," *The Times Picayune,* August 3, 1964; and "New Buildings at SLI Named for La. Natives," The Lafayette *Progress,* September 28, 1957.

[67]Lea Seale, Southwestern Louisiana Institute: History of the Institute Prepared for the Self-Evaluation Report for the Southern Association of Colleges and Secondary Schools, Lafayette, Louisiana, 1960, pp. 50-51.

[68]*Catalog,* 1959-60 as quoted by Seale.

[69]Lea Seale, Southwestern Louisiana Institute, pp. 50-51.

[70]*Catalog,* 1959-60, p. 50.

[71]Letter, Shelby M. Jackson to President Joel L. Fletcher, October 15, 1956, in U.S.L. Papers, Presidential Papers, 1900-58, S.A.M.C.

[72]*Southwestern Louisiana Institute: A Self Study,* 1958-59, Lafayette, Southwestern Louisiana Institute, 1958, p. 20.

[73]*Graduate School Catalog,* 1957-58, pp. 9-19.

[74]Clipping, "Graduate School has 116 Students For First Term," *The Vermilion,* October 11, 1957.

HISTORY OF UNIVERSITY OF SOUTHWESTERN LOUISIANA

[75]Clipping, "SLI to Offer Master's Degree in Three Additional Fields," *The Vermilion*, December 20, 1957.
[76]Clipping, "SLI Registrations Total 5,283; Highest in School's History," *The Daily Advertiser*, April 5, 1959.
[77]Clipping, "32 New Members Added to Faculty," *The Vermilion*, September 18, 1959.
[78]Clipping, "From Today on, It'll Be Known as USL," n.n., n.d., in U.S.L. Scrapbook, Louisiana Room Collection. Passage of the Bill: Senate 36-1; House of Representatives, 70-13.
[79]Clipping, "USL: Southwestern Declared a University, Accepted Bill Will Become Law July 27," *The Vermilion*, July 1, 1960.
[80]Clipping, "From Today On, It'll Be Known as USL," n.n., n.d., USL Scrapbook, Louisiana Room Collection.
[81]Joel L. Fletcher Papers, Speeches on USL, USL Papers, S.A.M.C.

CHAPTER VI
[1]Clipping, "Field Day at Lafayette," n.n., n.d., in U.S.L. Papers, Scrapbook, 1899-1907, p. 116.
[2]Clipping, "Interscholastic Athletic and Oratorical Association of Southwestern Louisiana; Constitution," n.n., n.d., in U.S.L. Papers, Scrapbook, 1902-1908, p. 5.
[3]Clipping, "Lafayette; Details Completed for Athletic Meet and Oratorical Contest," n.n., April 23, 1907, in U.S.L. Papers, Scrapbook, 1907-1908, p. 4.
[4]Clipping, "150 Schools Will Engage in Events at La. Institute," n.n., April 18, 1928, in U.S.L. Papers, Scrapbook, 1927-28, p. 74; Pamphlet IAOA Rallies and Tournaments, Southwestern Louisiana Institute, 1956. See Chapter I, The Formative Years for information concerning the beginning of the IAOA Rally.
[5]Clipping, "Athletic Association Organized," *The Vermilion*, February 8, 1909, p. 1.
[6]Letter, J. J. Vincent, President of "S" Club, to All Letter Men of SLI, July 14, 1922, in U.S.L. Papers, Presidential Papers, 1922.
[7]Clippings, "Southwestern Side-Lines Club is Forming; Banquet Set for Dec. 20th, n.n., n.d., in U.S.L. Papers, Scrapbook, 1927-28, p. 23; and "Greater Support for SLI Athletics Pledged at Side-Lines Banquet," n.n., n.d., in U.S.L. Papers, Scrapbook, 1927-28, p. 29.
[8]Clipping, "SLI Ticket Drive Under Full Swing," n.n., n.d., in U.S.L. Papers, Scrapbook, 1937-38, p. 2.
[9]Clipping, "S.L.I. Boosters Club is Formed to Help Bulldogs," The Beaumont *Enterprise*, September 14, 1940, in U.S.L. Papers, Scrapbook, 1940.
[10]Undated Memo of Clement J. McNaspy, Chairman of Committee on Boys Athletics, in U.S.L. Papers, Student Life, 1920; *Catalog, 1956-57, p. 43.*
[11]Editorial, "Pull for Southwestern," *The Daily Advertiser*, September 21, 1923, in U.S.L. Papers, Scrapbook, 1923-24.

158

[12]Clipping, "Commission Fears Too Much Athletics at SLI, Two Other Louisiana Colleges," n.n., Spring 1925, in U.S.L. Papers, Scrapbook, 1924-26.

[13]Clipping, "Referring to Surveys," n.n., January 28, 1925, in U.S.L. Papers, Scrapbook, 1924-26, p. 40.

[14]Clipping, "Gift by Jefferson Caffery to SLI Presented Today," n.n., n.d., in U.S.L. Papers, Scrapbook, 1923-24, p. 53; and Editorial by William M. Keefe, "Viewing the News; The Acorn grew," n.n., n.d., in U.S.L. Papers, Scrapbook, 1924-26, p. 106.

[15]Clipping, "Successful Campaign for Stadium at Southwestern Institute Came to Close Saturday with Over $37,000 Raised," n.n., Spring 1925, in U.S.L. Papers, Scrapbook, 1924-26, p. 106.

[16]Clipping, "$37,500 Raised for New Stadium in Three Hours," n.n., May 30, 1925, in U.S.L. Papers, Presidential Papers, 1925.

[17]Announcement, Quarter-Century Birthday Stadium for Southwestern Louisiana Institute, in U.S.L. Papers, Presidential Papers, 1925. The swimming pool was never completed.

[18]Clipping, "Ready for Dedication of SLI Stadium Friday," *The Daily Advertiser*, October 14, 1926, in U.S.L. Papers, Scrapbook, 1926-27, p. 128.

[19]Editorial, "Clement J. McNaspy," n.n., December 18, 1933, in U.S.L. Papers, Scrapbook, 1933-34; and Clipping, "Stadium at S.L.I. to be named After Clement J. McNaspy," *The Daily Advertiser*, March 19, 1940, in U.S.L. Papers, Scrapbook, 1940, McNaspy died December 18, 1933.

[20]Announcement, To the Patrons and Friends of Southwestern Institute from Ralph Squires, President of the Student Body, September 25, 1924, in U.S.L. Papers, Presidential Papers, 1924; and Clipping, "News received that Southwestern is Elected SIAA Member," n.n., Spring 1925, in U.S.L. Papers, Scrapbook, 1924-26, p. 36.

[21]Letter, Harry L. Griffin to Edwin L. Stephens, February 16, 1937, in U.S.L. Papers, Presidential Papers, 1937.

[22]Clipping, "Contract is Let for Gym at SLI," The Beaumont *Enterprise*, April 17, 1938, in U.S.L. Papers, Scrapbook, 1937-38, p. 121.

[23]Clipping, "New Gymnasium Opened at S.L.I.," *The Times Picayune*, January 9, 1939, in U.S.L. Papers, Scrapbook, 1938-39.

[24]Bob Henderson, ed. USL Football Program, 1967, University of Southwestern Louisiana, Lafayette, Louisiana, p. 8. Interview with Alexander G. Urban, July 9, 1968, Lafayette, Louisiana.

[25]Interview with Alexander G. Urban, July 9, 1968, Lafayette, Louisiana.

[26]Clipping, "Southern Wins Title; tech and SLI Runners-Up," The Crowley *Daily Signal*, November 22, 1948, in U.S.L. Papers, Scrapbook, 1948.

[27]Clipping, "S.L.I.I. 11, Crowley 5; Institute Defeated Crowley in Mud Ankle Deep," *The Vermilion*, November 11, 1907, p. 1.

[28]Clipping, "The St. Martin-Institute Football Game," *The Lafayette Gazette*, October 31, 1908, in U.S.L. Papers, Scrapbook, 1907-1908, p. 13.

[29]Letter, W. B. Hale, Manager L.I.I. to Manager, Football Team S.W. Industrial Institute, November 9, 1911, in U.S.L. Papers, Student Life, 1911.

[30]Letter, (Secretary & Treasurer) to Mr. M. D. Fridge, Mgr. Baton Rouge High School Football Team, September 8, 1909, in U.S.L. Papers, Student Life, 1909.

[31]Letter, H. J. Stahl, President Southwestern Louisiana Industrial Institute Athletic Association to Friends of SLII, December 1, 1917, in U.S.L. Papers, Scrapbook, 1917-18, p. 68.

[32]Announcement, Proposed Football Schedule, 1918, in U.S.L. Papers, Student Life, 1918.

[33]Clipping, "Southwestern Football Schedule for 1923," n.n., n.d., in U.S.L. Papers, Scrapbook, 1923-24, p. 13.

[34]Clipping, "Tulane and LSU Dropped from SLI Schedule," n.n., n.d., in U.S.L. Papers, Scrapbook, 1931-32, p. 5.

[35]Clipping, "Introduce Night Football here," *The Lafayette Tribune*, November 5, 1931, in U.S.L. Papers, Scrapbook, 1931-32, p. 131.

[36]Clippings, "S.L.I. Ranks Among Top Team Winning Six Straight Games," *The Daily Advertiser*, November 24, 1938, in U.S.L. Papers, Scrapbook, 1938, p. 93; and Kaliste Saloom, Jr. "Bulldogs Turn in Uniforms After Very Successful Season," *The Daily Advertiser*, November 30, 1938, in U.S.L. Papers, Scrapbook, 1938, p. 124.

[37]Clipping, "Abel Placed on the First All SIAA Team," *The Daily Advertiser*, December 12, 1938, in U.S.L. Papers, Scrapbook, 1938, p. 131.

[38]Clipping, "Five Louisiana Schools Form Conference," The Beaumont *Enterprise*, September 11, 1939, in U.S.L. Papers, Scrapbook, 1939, p. 69.

[39]Clipping, "Bulldogs Defeat La. Normal to Win L.I.C. Title," *The Daily Advertiser*, November 29, 1940, in U.S.L. Papers, Scrapbook, 1940.

[40]Clipping, "Southeastern Admitted to Louisiana Conference," *The Shreveport Times*, May 12, 1940, in U.S.L. Papers, Scrapbook, 1940.

[41]Souvenir Program of First Annual Oil Bowl, January 1, 1944, in U.S.L. Papers, Presidential Papers, 1900-58.

[42]Clippings, "Institute Notes; Students Assisting in Advertising Coming of the Cincinnati Reds," n.n., n.d.; "Cincinnati Reds Play Institute; Score 13 to 1 Favor Visitors – Institute Plays Good Game," n.n., n.d., in U.S.L. Papers, Scrapbook, 1914-15, p. 18, 21; "C. J. Alias Cincinnati Reds, Will Be Mascot," in U.S.L. Papers, Scrapbook, 1915-16, p. 39.

[43]Clipping, "Southwestern Institute Has Given Up Baseball This Year Except for Games Among the Class Teams," n.n., n.d., in U.S.L. Papers, Scrapbook, 1927-28, p. 55.

[44]Clipping, "S.L.I. Will Resume Baseball Activities," n.n., n.d., in U.S.L. Papers, Scrapbook, 1938-39.

[45]Clipping, "SLI Baseballers Preparing for 22-Game Slate," The Beaumont Enterprise, March 9, 1940, in U.S.L. Papers, Scrapbook, 1940.

[46]L'Acadien, 1956, p. 231.

[47]Letter, C. J. McNaspy to Principal E. S. Jenkins, Lake Charles, January 20, 1912, in U.S.L. Papers, Student Life, 1912.

[48]L'Acadien, 1956, p. 230.

[49]Clipping, "Southwestern Introduces Student Boxing, January 22," n.n., n.d., in U.S.L. Papers, Scrapbook, 1930-31, p. 1.

[50]Clipping, "5200 Watch S.L.I. Boxers Battle L.S.U.," The Beaumont Enterprise, February 21, 1939, in U.S.L. Papers, Scrapbook, 1938-39.

[51]Clipping, "Bulldog Mittmen Prepare for Hard 1940 Boxing Schedule," The Daily Advertiser, December 12, 1939, in Scrapbook, 1939-40.

[52]Clipping, "Bellaire Captures Nat'l Crown," The Morning Advocate, March 30, 1941, in U.S.L. Papers, Scrapbook, 1941. Interview with Alexander G. Urban, July 9, 1968, Lafayette, Louisiana.

[53]Clipping, "Golf Team to be Formed at Southwestern," The Daily Advertiser, March 3, 1939, in U.S.L. Papers, Scrapbook, 1938-39.

[54]Clipping, "S.L.I. Defeats La. Normal in Golf Game," The Daily Advertiser, April 20, 1940, in U.S.L. Papers, Scrapbook, 1940.

[55]Clipping, "400 Athletes to be Here Saturday for SLI Relays," n.n., n.d., in U.S.L. Papers, Scrapbook, 1927-28, p. 58.

[56]Interview with E. Glynn Abel, July 15, 1968, Lafayette, Louisiana.

[57]Undated Announcement, Southwestern Hall of Fame, Drayton Lewis, Southwestern Hall of Fame Committee Member.

[58]USL Football Program, 1967, p. 34.

[59]Clipping, "Gymnasts Will go to Crowley on Tuesday," The Daily Advertiser, March 18, 1940, in U.S.L. Papers, Scrapbook, 1940.

[60]Clipping, "S.L.I. Sports Year Declared One of Best in School History," The Daily Advertiser, June 3, 1941, in U.S.L. Papers, Scrapbook, 1941.

[61]Annual Report of the Department of Athletics, Southwestern Louisiana Institute, 1941-42, in U.S.L. Papers, Presidential Papers, 1900-58.

[62]Clipping, "6 Louisiana Colleges Cut Out Athletics," The Times Picayune, January 12, 1943, in U.S.L. Papers, Scrapbook, 1942-43.

[63]Pamphlet, The Intramural Program for Men, 1950-51, in U.S.L. Papers, Presidential papers, 1900-58.

CHAPTER VII

[1]Letter, W. O. Martin, Commandment of Cadets to Edwin L. Stephens, January 10, 1907, in U.S.L. Papers, Student Life, 1907. See Chapter I, The Formative Years, for more information on military discipline at Southwestern.

[2]Letter, James Byrns to Edwin L. Stephens, January 12, 1911, in U.S.L. Papers, Student Life, 1911.

[3]Letters, Edwin L. Stephens to Mrs. P. Ravia, June 22, 1914; and Edwin L. Stephens to Mr. A. L. Jewell, February 19, 1917, in U.S.L. Papers, Student Life, 1917.

[4]Interview with A. Wilmot Dalferes, July 9, 1968, Lafayette, Louisiana.

[5]Memo, Some Boarding Club Rules for Summer School Students, 1909, in U.S.L. Papers, Presidential Papers, 1909.

[6]Announcement, Library Rules, in U.S.L. Papers, Student Life, 1909.

[7]Clipping, "Use of Tobacco Prohibited at Lafayette Industrial," n.n., March 8, 1906, in U.S.L. Papers, Scrapbook, 1899-1907.

[8]Letters, Edwin L. Stephens to Mr. Harry Curley, August 9, 1910; and Edwin L. Stephens to Mr. Roy Cookston, August 31, 1910, in U.S.L. Papers, Student Life, 1910.

[9]Clippings, "Gets Army Camp at Southwestern," n.n., n.d.; "War Department Wants Training Camps for Boys," n.n., n.d., in U.S.L. Papers, Scrapbook, 1917-18, p. 61, 63; and Letter, Edwin L. Stephens to the Alumni, Former Students and Friends of the Southwest Louisiana Industrial Institute, September 25, 1918, in U.S.L. Papers, Presidential Papers, 1918.

[10]Letter, (President, Louisiana) to Edwin L. Stephens, December 2, 1918, in U.S.L. Papers, Presidential Papers, 1919.

[11]Clipping, "Students to Aid the Local Board," n.n., n.d., in U.S.L. Papers, Scrapbook, 1915-16, p. 28.

[12]Clipping, "SLII Notes," n.n., n.d., in U.S.L. Papers, Scrapbook, 1917-18, p. 73.

[13]Clipping, "Institute Pays Heroes Tribute," *The Daily Advertiser*, January 9, 1920, in U.S.L. Papers, Presidential Papers, 1920.

[14]*Catalog*, 1921, pp. 18-19.

[15]*Ibid.*

[16]Memo by Miss Edith G. Dupré, May 19, 1923, in U.S.L. Papers, Presidential Papers, 1923.

[17]Pamphlet, *Student's Handbook of Southwestern Louisiana Institute*, Published and presented by the Newman Club, 1924-25, pp. 6-41. See Chapter I, The Formative Years, for more information on early extra-curricular activities.

[18]Clippings, "Probe Under Way of Hair Cutting at Southwestern," n.n., n.d.; and "Freshmen at SLI Lose Shining Locks in Hazing Stunts," n.n., April 17, 1929, in U.S.L. Papers, Scrapbook, 1929-30, p. 66.

[19]Clippings, "Student Dismissals Result of Southwestern 'Hair Clipping'," n.n., n.d.; and "Five Dismissed as Hair Clipping Quiz Continues," n.n., April 25, 1929, in U.S.L. Papers, Scrapbook, 1929-30, p. 63-64.

[20]Student Handbook, 1938-39, pp. 10-11, in U.S.L. Papers, Presidential Papers, 1900-58.

[21]Clipping, "Contract Awarded on Student Center," *The Times Picayune*, March 17, 1938, in U.S.L. Papers, Scrapbook, 1937-38, p. 87.

[22]Clipping, "Southwestern at War," The St. Martinville *Weekly Messenger*, August 7, 1942, in U.S.L. Papers, Scrapbook, 1942.

[23]Clippings, "V-1 Program Will Prolong College Career," n.n., April 21, 1942, in U.S.L. Papers, Scrapbook, 1941; and "1200 From S.L.I. With the Armed Forces," *The Daily Advertiser*, April 22, 1943, in U.S.L. Papers, Scrapbook, 1942-43; Interview with Joseph Riehl, June 19, 1968, Lafayette, Louisiana.

[24]Clippings, "Housing of Veterans Returning to College Under GI Bill of Rights is Problem of Serious Proportions, Education Board Told," The Crowley *Daily Signal*, January 18, 1946, in U.S.L. Papers, Scrapbook, 1946-47; and "Breakdown of Courses Pursued by Veterans," Fall, 1946, in U.S.L. Papers, Presidential Papers, 1900-58.

[25]Letter, Olney Place, Lt. Col., Inf. U.S.A. Acting District Military Inspector to Edwin L. Stephens, July 14, 1919, in U.S.L. Papers, Presidential Papers, 1919.

[26]Letter, Lether E. Frazar to Commanding General Fourth Corps Area, January 18, 1939, in U.S.L. Papers, Presidential Papers, 1900-58; and Clipping, "Move is Started for R.O.T.C. Unit in Southwestern," September 19, 1940, in U.S.L. Papers, Scrapbook, 1940.

[27]Clipping, "SLI Students to be Offered Air Reserve Officer Training," *The Beauregard News*, December 23, 1948, in U.S.L. Papers, Scrapbook, 1914.

[28]Memo, Committee on Student Publications to the President and Faculty, n.d., in U.S.L. Papers, Student Life, 1914.

[29]Clipping, "National Contest Won by Vermilion," *The Times Picayune*, June 7, 1939, in U.S.L. Papers, Scrapbook, 1939, p. 6.

[30]Letter, Edwin L. Stephens to Hon. Robert Martin, March 27, 1912, in U.S.L. Papers, Presidential Papers, 1912.

[31]Pamphlet, *Student's Handbook of Southwestern Louisiana Institute*, Published and Presented by the Newman Club, 1924-25, p. 40.

[32]Memo, Harry L. Griffin, Chairman of Students' Publications Committee to Edwin L. Stephens, May 22, 1919, in U.S.L. Papers, Presidential Papers, 1919.

[33]Clipping, "First Issue of Literary Script is Published," *The Daily Advertiser*, December 1, 1939, in U.S.L. Papers, Scrapbook, 1939-40; Student Publication of *Exile*, 1956. Dupré Library is named in honor of Edith Garland Dupré's family.

[34]Clipping, "Handbook Now Ready for S.L.I. Student Body," *The Daily Advertiser*, August 28, 1939, in U.S.L. Papers, Scrapbook, 1939, p. 62.

[35]Memo, Report of Faculty Committee on Student Employment, in U.S.L. Papers, Presidential Papers, 1931.

[36]Clippings, "Lafayette Institute Beats Louisiana Record in Giving Training to Sons of Poor Farm Families;" and "Work Progressing on SLI Dormitory," n.n., n.d., in U.S.L. Papers, Scrapbook, 1936-37, pp. 50, 121.

[37]Clipping, "New Dormitory at SLI Assured," The Beaumont *Enterprise*, November 1, 1937, in U.S.L. Papers, Scrapbook, 1938, p. 8.

[38]E. W. Stagg, "College on $13 a Month," *The Progressive Farmer,* May 1938, in U.S.L. Papers, Scrapbook, 1938, p. 8.

[39]Clipping, "Southwest Louisiana Students Grow their own Food," n.n., n.d., in U.S.L. Papers, Scrapbook, 1935-36.

[40]Clipping, "S.L.I. Placement Service is Being Formed," *The Daily Advertiser*, April 16, 1941, in U.S.L. Papers, Scrapbook, 1941.

[41]Clipping, "Plans Formed Raise Funds for Center," *The Daily Advertiser*, October 2, 1937, in U.S.L. Papers, Scrapbook, 1937-38, p. 15.

[42]Clipping, "Newman Club Meeting Held Thursday S.L.I.," *The Daily Advertiser*, September 28, 1940, in U.S.L. Papers, Scrapbook, 1940.

[43]Clipping, "$50,000 Center For Catholic Students of SLI to be Built," *The Beaumont Enterprise*, April 12, 1941, in U.S.L. Papers, Scrapbook, 1941.

[44]Clipping, "First Mass at S.L.I. Center on March 1st," *The Daily Advertiser*, February 24, 1942, in U.S.L. Papers, Scrapbook, 1942.

[45]Clipping, "Make Plans for Union Party to be Saturday," *The Daily Advertiser*, September 28, 1940, in U.S.L. Papers, Scrapbook, 1940.

[46]Clipping, "Five Religious Groups at S.L.I.," The Lafayette *Progress*, September 4, 1941, in U.S.L. Papers, Scrapbook, 1941.

[47]Letter, Edwin L. Stephens to Hon. Lorris M. Wimberly, Secretary, Louisiana Tax Reform Commission, July 26, 1933, in U.S.L. Papers, Presidential Papers, 1933.

[48]Clipping, "Pledging Held by S.L.I. Sorority Mon.," *The Daily Advertiser,* October 8, 1940, in U.S.L. Papers, Scrapbook, 1940.

[49]Clippings, "S.L.I. Organizes Phi Kappa Theta," *The Times Picayune*, January 15, 1939, in U.S.L. Papers, Scrapbook, 1938-39; and "Nat'l Catholic Fraternity will Have S.L.I. Unit," in the Lafayette *Progress,* March 27, 1941, in U.S.L. Papers, Scrapbook, 1941.

[50]Handbook, 1956-57, pp. 30-33; *L'Acadien*, 1956, pp. 176-191; *L'Acadien* 1962, 143-177; and Bradley Quoyser, ed. *Introducing Fraternities at S.L.I.*, 1956-57, Lafayette: Southwestern Louisiana Institute, 1956, pp. 15-20.

[51]Letter, B. C. Riley, National Blue Key President, to Edwin L. Stephens, April 12, 1932, in U.S.L. Papers, Presidential Papers, 1932.

[52]Clipping, "Chapter of Blue Key Fraternity Secured at SLI," n.n., n.d., in U.S.L. Papers, Scrapbook, 1932-33, p. 29.

[53]Clipping, n.n., n.d., in U.S.L. Papers, Scrapbook, 1938, p. 80.

[54]Clipping, "SLI Club Opened for Day Students," *The Times Picayune*, October 16, 1937, in U.S.L. Papers, Scrapbook, 1937-38, p. 17.

[55]Clipping, "Installation of Alpha Phi Omega Fraternity at S.L.I. Announced," *The Daily Advertiser*, February 24, 1939, in U.S.L. Papers, 1938-39.

[56]Clippings, "Puerto Ricans at S.L.I. Form Club," *The Times Picayune*, February 19, 1939, in U.S.L. Papers, Scrapbook, 1938-39; and "Latin Club of Southwestern Elects Officers," *The Daily Advertiser*, May 28, 1940, in U.S.L. Papers, Scrapbook, 1940.

[57]Clipping, "National Honor Fraternity was formed at SLI," n.n., n.d., in U.S.L. Papers, Scrapbook, 1940.

[58]Clipping, "Honor Society Formed at SLI," n.n., n.d., in U.S.L. Papers, Scrapbook, 1935-36.
[59]Clippings, "Winter Concert Announced at SLI," *The Times Picayune*, December 6, 1948, in U.S.L. Papers, Scrapbook, 1948; and "History Society to be Organized on SLI Campus," *The Vermilion*, October 22, 1954.
[60]Letter, Edwin L. Stephens to Hon. Lorris M. Wimberly, Secretary, Louisiana Tax Reform Commission, July 26, 1933, in U.S.L. Papers, Presidential papers, 1933.
[61]Clipping, "SLI be first in La. to Get Engr. Chapter," *The Daily Advertiser*, January 12, 1949, in U.S.L. Papers, Scrapbook, 1949.
[62]Clipping, "Average S.L.I. Man Described After Survey," *The Daily Advertiser*, July 8, 1940, in U.S.L. Papers, Scrapbook, 1940.
[63]*Handbook*, 1956-57, pp. 30-33; *L'Acadien*, 1956, pp. 176-191; and Bradley Quoyser, ed. *Introducing Fraternitites at S.L.I., 1956-57*, Lafayette: Southwestern Louisiana Institute, 1956, pp. 15-20.

CHAPTER VIII

[1]Editorial, "'Sharing' Among Universities," *The Daily Advertiser*, April 19, 1964, Joel L. Fletcher Papers, S.A.M.C.
[2]Interview with Joel L. Fletcher, March 20, 1969. Clyde L. Rougeau was acting president from January 1, 1966 until June 30, 1966.
[3]Margaret Dixon, "USL Mapping Plans to Use Iberia Base," *The Morning Advocate*, October 30, 1964, Joel L. Fletcher Papers, S.A.M.C.
[4]Clipping, "USL Accepts Base," *The Daily Advertiser*, June 15, 1965, Joel L. Fletcher Papers, S.A.M.C. This was an interim permit. The United States General Services Administration presented the base to the Louisiana State Board of Education and USL at a later date.
[5]Clipping, "USL Iberia Proposal Assailed by Critics," *The Daily Advertiser*, August 4, 1965, in Joel L. Fletcher Papers, S.A.M.C.
[6]Clipping, "Fletcher, Board Vary on Transfer to Iberia," *The Daily Advertiser*, August 11, 1965, in Joel L. Fletcher Papers, S.A.M.C.
[7]Letter, Lafayette Chamber of Commerce to Hon. W. E. Whetstone, President, Louisiana Board of Education, September 8, 1965, in Joel L. Fletcher Papers, S.A.M.C.
[8]Letter, Murial McCulla Price to the Lafayette *Advertiser*, September 8, 1965, Joel L. Fletcher Papers, S.A.M.C.
[9]Clippings, "USL President Resigns Office," *The Times Picayune*, October 17, 1965; and "Joel Fletcher Resigns USL Presidency," *The Morning Advocate*, October 17, 1965; "Board Okays USL N.I.; Fletcher Quits Post," *The Daily Advertiser*, October 17, 1965, Joel L. Fletcher Papers, S.A.M.C.
[10]Clipping, "Rougeau is officially named head of USL," *The Vermilion*, July 8, 1966. [11]Editorial, "Irresponsible Board Action," *The Daily Advertiser*, October 24, 1965, Joel L. Fletcher Papers, S.A.M.C.
[12]Brochure, Recommendations Relative to the Establishment of the Education Center of the University of Southwestern Louisiana, November 5, 1965, p. 2. Joel L. Fletcher Papers, S.A.M.C. Courses to

be offered in Freshman course toward bachelors: English, mathematics, social studies, science, electives, physical education or air science, and orientation, p. 9. The Department of Technical Studies: Associate degrees in agricultural engineering, air conditioning and refrigeration, chemical, civil, construction, data processing, dental, drafting, electronics, herdsman, instrumentation, law enforcement, machine, medical, metal fabrication, nursery management, nursing, office services, mechanical power, restaurant management and turfgrass management, p. 12.

[13]Clipping, "Suit Filed Today Against USL Move," *The Daily Advertiser*, December 10, 1965, Joel L. Fletcher Papers, S.A.M.C.

[14]Full Text of Decision, *The Daily Advertiser*, March 25, 1966, Joel L. Fletcher Papers, March 25, 1966, S.A.M.C.

[15]*Ibid.*

[16]Clipping, "USL in Iberia Plan Blocked," *The Daily Advertiser*, February 20, 1967, in Joel L. Fletcher Papers, S.A.M.C.

INDEX

*This Index does not include the Appendices and Footnotes.

M

INDEX

121, 124, 125

www.ingramcontent.com/pod-product-compliance
Lightning Source LLC
Chambersburg PA
CBHW071401160426
42812CB00085B/1071